Contents

I The Health Policy Landscape: Shifting Perspectives on Costs, Quality, and Access 1
Stanley B. Jones

Appendix: Health Care Statistics 12

II Policymaking for Health Care Delivery: 1990 Review and Prospects for 1991 19
C. Ross Anthony

III Economic Indicators of Health Care Problems 43
with Commentaries by J. Richard Gaintner and W. Douglas Skelton

IV Public Dissatisfaction with Health Care 51
with Commentaries by Ronald P. Kaufman and Paul E. Stanton, Jr.

V Proposals to Reform the Health Care Delivery System 59
with Commentaries by Ronald P. Kaufman and Richard L. O'Brien

Health

CURRENT ISSUES AND THE

Care

PUBLIC POLICY DEBATE

Delivery

Ronald Kaufman
John Naughton
Marian Osterweis
Elaine Rubin
Editors

Association of Academic Health Centers

The Association of Academic Health Centers (AHC) is a national, non-profit organization comprising more than 100 institutional members in the United States and Canada. The AHC is dedicated to improving the health of the people through leadership and cooperative action with others. The AHC seeks to influence public dialogue on significant health and science policy issues, to advance education for health professionals, to promote biomedical and health services research, and to enhance patient care. The AHC commitment is embodied in the traditional university values of knowledge, integrity, innovation, and intellectual freedom.

The views expressed in this book are those of its authors and do not necessarily represent the views of the Board of Directors of the Association of Academic Health Centers or the membership at large.

The Association of Academic Health Centers
Washington, D.C.

© 1991 by the Association of Academic Health Centers
All rights reserved. Published 1991
Printed in the United States of America

Library of Congress Catalog Card Number: 91-72677
ISBN 1-879694-01-8 19.95
ISSN 1056-2389

Copies of this book may be purchased from:
Association of Academic Health Centers
1400 Sixteenth Street, N.W.
Suite 410
Washington, D.C. 20036
202/265-9600
Fax: 202/265-7514

Price: $19.95 plus $3.00 postage and handling.

Design and Production: Fletcher Design, Washington, D.C.

HEALTH POLICY ANNUAL I
Health Care Delivery
EDITORIAL ADVISORY BOARD

Robert J. Joynt, M.D., Ph.D.
Vice President and Vice Provost for
  Health Affairs
University of Rochester Medical
  Center

Ronald P. Kaufman, M.D.
Vice President for Health Sciences
University of South Florida

Peter O. Kohler, M.D.
President
Oregon Health Sciences University
Associate Chairman

John N. Lein, M.D.
Vice President for Health Sciences
University of Washington

M. David Low, M.D., Ph.D.
President
The University of Texas Health
  Science Center at Houston

Leon S. Malmud, M.D.
Vice President for the Health
  Sciences Center
Temple University

Richard A. Matré, Ph.D.
Vice President for the Medical
  Center
St. Louis University

Russell L. Miller, Jr., M.D.
Vice President for Health Affairs
Howard University

James E. Mulvihill, D.M.D.
Vice President and Provost for
  Health Affairs and Executive
  Director
University of Connecticut Health
  Center

John Naughton, M.D.
Vice President for Clinical Affairs
  and Dean, School of Medicine
  and Biomedical Sciences
State University of New York at
  Buffalo
Chairman

Richard L. O'Brien, M.D.
Vice President for Health Sciences
Creighton University

Clayton Rich, M.D.
Provost and Vice President for
  Health Sciences, Oklahoma City
  Campus
University of Oklahoma

Perry G. Rigby, M.D.
Chancellor
Louisiana State University Medical
  Center

Richard D. Ruppert, M.D.
President
Medical College of Ohio

David Satcher, M.D., Ph.D.
President
Meharry Medical College

Donald J. Scherl, M.D.
President
State University of New York
  Health Science Center at Booklyn

W. Douglas Skelton, M.D.
Provost for Medical Affairs
Dean, School of Medicine
Mercer University

Paul E. Stanton, Jr., M.D.
Vice President for Health Affairs
  and Dean, James H. Quillen
  College of Medicine
East Tennessee State University

Francis J. Tedesco, M.D.
President
Medical College of Georgia

Joseph P. Van Der Meulen, M.D.
Vice President, Health Affairs
University of Southern California

Others

C. Ross Anthony, Ph.D.
Principal
Health Policy Alternatives, Inc.

Roger J. Bulger, M.D.
President
Association of Academic Health
  Centers

Arthur L. Caplan, Ph.D.
Director, Center for Biomedical
  Ethics
Professor, Department of Philoso-
  phy and Professor, Department of
  Surgery
University of Minnesota

Henry R. Desmarais, M.D.
Principal
Health Policy Alternatives, Inc.

Phillip M. Forman, M.D.
Director
Center for Health Services Research
University of Illinois at Chicago

Marsha Gold, Sc.D.
Director, Research and Analysis
Group Health Association of
  America, Inc.

Ruth S. Hanft, Ph.D.
Consultant and Visiting Professor
The George Washington University

Stanley B. Jones
Health Policy Consultant

Michael L. Millman, Ph.D.
Senior Staff Officer
Institute of Medicine
National Academy of Sciences

Marian Osterweis, Ph.D.
Vice President
Association of Academic Health
  Centers

Elaine R. Rubin, Ph.D.
Program Associate
Association of Academic Health
  Centers

Norman W. Weissman, Ph.D.
Director
Center for General Health Services
Extramural Research
Agency for Health Care Policy and
  Research

Tables

Illustrations

Preface

This book is the culmination of the work of the Task Force on Health Care Delivery of the Association of Academic Health Centers, a group that for the past three years has been seriously studying public policy issues related to the financing, costs, quality, and access to health care services. The publication is in a sense frozen in time, providing a snapshot of critical health care delivery issues—from indigent care to international comparisons, from reimbursement to rationing, and from Medicare to Medicaid—for the period 1989-1990. This volume is a compilation of abstracts and excerpts of significant articles and reports along with commentaries written by members of the task force and the editorial advisory board. Those writings selected by the editorial advisory board for inclusion in this volume present a wide array of issues and myriad viewpoints on longstanding and emerging problems in the American health care system and ways to resolve them. All the selections were deemed important for their focus on issues and activities that signal change and transformation in health care policy in the coming years. In this sense, this is a timely and relevant reference for anyone interested in health care policy issues.

The commentaries are unique. The authors, chief executive officers of academic health centers throughout the country, address these selected health policy issues from broad, interdisciplinary perspectives that take account of complex and often conflicting goals and missions within the health care delivery system in the United States. Some commentaries reflect personal and institutional experiences and the day-to-day realities of health care delivery in academic health centers; others provide new insights on specific issues such as financing or rationing of care by relating the national experience to particular regional or local problems.

These commentaries are not meant to resolve the many dilemmas that face policymakers and practitioners in the health care arena. Rather the authors seek to enhance and enrich the public policy debate during this period of important evolution and transformation in health care policy and practice.

This volume is the first in a series of health policy annuals that will be published by the Association of Academic Health Centers. In future editions, the themes may vary. However, the format will remain the same, with each volume providing an array of selected writings that are pivotal to the development and transformation of health care policy in the United States.

Ronald P. Kaufman
John Naughton
Marian Osterweis
Elaine R. Rubin

CHAPTER I

The Health Policy Landscape

Shifting Perspectives on Costs, Quality, and Access

Stanley B. Jones

T here is a growing sense of urgency among policymakers, employers, insurers, and the public about the seemingly incompatible need to resolve problems of access to health care services for America's uninsured and underinsured populations and to control costs without threatening the quality of care.

It is not merely the dawn of a new decade that sparks concerns about health care policies and heightens interest in reassessing the nature of health care delivery in this country. Rather, there is widespread recognition that major transformations in the social and economic fabric of America have profoundly affected public perceptions and expectations about the role of health care in American society and the nature of a vast network of health care delivery that has been labeled, though perhaps euphemistically, as the American health care "system."

This monograph highlights the major currents of the public policy debate that characterized the health care arena during 1989 and 1990. This volume includes abstracts and excerpts of significant articles on health care delivery issues that were published during these years, along with commentaries by the members of the Task Force on Health Care Delivery of the Association of Academic Health Centers (AHC).

The AHC group, comprising more than 30 chief executive officers of academic health centers throughout the nation, has been monitoring significant policy questions related to access, quality of care, and health care financing for more than three years.

In part, the articles were selected because they attempt to bridge two decades, thus reflecting forces of change and perhaps signaling new directions in health policy. Both this chapter and the one that follows decribe the historical context of the current policy debates, review recent congressional activity, and forecast likely health policy action for the future. In the commentaries that accompany each chapter, task force members react to the selected articles, often relating the issues to experiences at the academic health centers as well as events at the national level.

Some people now believe that there are basic defects in the structure, financing, and quality of this chaotic, fragmented, complex array of programs for patient care and treatment. There is a growing concern that millions of Americans are excluded from the system and that crises are imminent as the gap between America's rich and poor continues to widen (see figure A.1, table A.1, and table A.2). These issues have acquired added urgency in light of major demographic changes in the United States, including our aging population, and a rising tide of poverty and disease.

These concerns are not new. Since the early 1960s, public policy-makers have turned again and again to health issues and the need to improve health care delivery in the United States. The debate has revolved around three interrelated questions: (1) What is our societal obligation in ensuring access and how can we fulfill that obligation? (2) How can we ensure acceptable quality of health care? and (3) How can we keep the costs of care affordable for both the individual and society?

Over the decades these questions have emerged with varying degrees of intensity and differing points of focus. In the 1960s and early 1970s there was an emphasis on increased government involvement in an attempt to provide greater access to more health care services.

A primary objective of the policies in the 1960s and early 1970s was to take steps to expand access to comprehensive health services. We saw the enactment of Medicare and Medicaid and strengthening of grant programs to extend services to poor and rural communities, the mentally ill, and low-income pregnant women and children. During this era there were also grants to institutions for the training of health professionals, loan programs for students in the health professions, and a continuation of grants to hospitals to expand services.

Throughout the 1970s public policy debates on various national health insurance proposals were continually fueled by the political interest in expanding access to health services for all Americans. At the same time, however, the increasing costs of public programs and private health benefits focused attention on constraining the rate of increase in spending. These included efforts to constrain Medicare and Medicare spending, the Nixon administration's wage and price controls, a number of state hospital rate-setting programs, and a national debate on hospital cost containment. In addition, there was increased attention to constrain spending in one form or another through mechanisms as diverse as health planning, professional standards review, and health maintenance organizations (HMOs).

In the early 1980s there was a continuation of the shift in emphasis to the issue of costs, a factor that for the 1990s appears to have grown to an obsession. The focus was on the federal share of expenditures. More sophisticated services, increased training of health care professionals, the growth in the numbers of hospitals, major advances in technology, and the expansion of public and private insurance programs helped to fuel tremendous increases in health care costs. Under the Reagan administration, the government began to dismantle some system-wide regulatory programs and focused directly on how to cut the still rising costs of the national Medicare and Medicaid programs.

For the 1990s, the currents of reform appear stronger than ever, with more visible tensions between those who argue for sweeping reform that would force a major overhaul of the system and those who would continue an incremental approach to change. New perspectives on quality and the value of services have emerged, and health care providers are under greater pressure to analyze and evaluate the effectiveness and outcomes of health care. Concerns about costs are now driving many people to examine the allocation of resources and openly advocate formalized rationing of health care services. Finally, there are more general signs of public dissatisfaction, reflected in part by a renewed interest in examining health care systems in Canada and Europe that might serve as models in this country.

In general, the strategies for reform that were proposed during these decades strongly reflected changes in the political thinking of the era. The 1960s focused on government-sponsored health care programs for the aged and poor. Economic issues entered the public policy debates of the 1970s and focused on government regulation of the supply and price of services. Decision-making in the 1980s was oriented to the payers with both the government and the private sector seeking to limit the rate of increase in its share of spending. A new perspective on health care based on market-oriented reforms, competition and privately-organized managed care programs emerged. In the late 1980s, proposals for reform tended to represent a patchwork of policies; they combined market-based reform elements with expansions of public insurance, mandates for private insurance and government regulation of the insurance market.

However, the 1990s finds policymakers despairing about the effectiveness of either regulation or competition as a viable means to control total systemwide costs. There is also a perception that cost containment measures may have taken their toll on quality. There is mounting concern that the much praised market-oriented system of health services has not and cannot fairly or equitably serve the American population, particularly the poor.

Economic Indicators and Public Dissatisfaction

Economic forces, whether or not they were aided by policy, brought about many of these changes in the design and structure of health care delivery. Regardless of the cause—advances in technology and medicine, fees for physicians, decreased hospital reimbursement or the competitive marketplace—health care expenditures continue to grow (see figure A.2). For example, from 1980-1989 the health sector's share of the gross national product increased from 9.1 percent to 11.6 percent (see table A.3). National health expenditures continued to rise at double digit rates, increasing by more than 15 percent in those years, from $249 billion to $604 billion (see table A.4). With a 10 percent annual rate of increase, the nation's health care expenditures are projected to more than double by the year 2000, with total spending reaching well over $1 trillion.

The federal government's Medicare program has seen one of the most rapid increases in expenditures since 1970. From 1975 to 1990, federal outlays for Medicare rose more than 650 percent; these increases are mirrored in state expenditures for Medicaid (see table A.5).

Health insurance premiums for employers greatly increased, often by more than 20 percent; these increases are projected to continue in the coming year. With these rates of increase, health benefits are consuming a greater share of corporate budgets.

Some corporations have expressed grave concerns over rising health care costs, pointing out that such costs are threatening the ability of American business to compete in the international marketplace. One private sector response was to develop alternative health programs to offer their employees, and thus help to reduce costs. Health maintenance organizations enjoyed new popularity during the 1980s, and now offer the "managed care" concept to millions of people in the workforce.

But there is a growing suspicion among employers and insurers that multiple choice systems of health insurance are not containing costs. The vast majority now have such multiple options. The hope was that HMOs would in some way constrain future premium increases and/or allow employers to give better benefits to their employees for the same outlays. However, many employers are not convinced of this strategy. In fact, the problem of adverse selection may actually be increasing employers' premium costs in these multiple choice systems, thus undercutting a fundamental goal of the competitive approach to containing health care costs that drove health policy in the 1980s.

This seeming failure of competing health plans to contain costs is of great importance. The demise of the market-based multiple choice approach to cost containment could open the way to a more standardized and centrally-managed system of health care. One possible private market alternative to multiple choice is a more monolithic system under the control of one employer, either directly or through an insurer. The public policy alternative is standardization of payment mechanisms and tighter regulation; such an example would be an extension of the new Medicare physician payment system to all payers.

Employers have also shifted more of the costs of care to their employees, thus reducing the employer's expenses for health insurance. Some employers have suggested that it may no longer be feasible for them to finance employee health insurance. What was once a rather simple matter of offering financial protection for employees has become a complex process of choosing doctors and hospitals for employees and their families.

Dissatisfaction with the delivery of health care services does not end with employers and the government. It extends to health care providers and patients as well. Providers and patients are showing signs of increasing dissatisfaction with the intrusive and cumbersome and confusing environment surrounding insurance mechanisms and, ultimately the provision of care. Providers and patients alike are angered and frustrated by rising costs.

Large numbers of health care professionals still believe that the clinical management of the patient is their professional and legal responsibility, a philosophy that in many ways runs counter to the managed care concept. Many physicians view efforts to manage care as harassment and interference by third parties in the practice of medicine.

Given that health care affects the lives of all Americans, public opinion can set the tone or direction for any major national decision. While public opinion has generally favored universal access, recent history reveals that the public placed other issues, including some social reform, the economy, and defense higher on its list of priorities. While there were calls to address specific issues, such as rising costs, there was generally little public enthusiasm for any one particular solution. An interest in equity in access to health care services that was eclipsed when concerns about costs took center stage appears to have reemerged.

Thus, a hallmark of the 1990s may be more organized public support and interest in reform. Public attitudes appear to be changing as evidenced by calls for greater patient involvement in decision-making with health care practitioners, renewed concerns for the poor, and increasing public interest in health promotion and disease prevention activities. It remains to be seen whether public opinion polls translate into public policy or whether any health care proposals can gain public support and endorsement for the 1990s.

Proposals to Reform the Health Care Delivery System

The public policy debate on health care and the reform proposals that have come forward over the last few decades point up differing philosophies about the roles and responsibilities of federal and state governments and the private sector. In addition, the solutions advocated at the federal level to achieve greater access and control costs have varied over time, including universal coverage, regulation, and competition, along with federal incentives related to the structuring or financing of health care delivery.

Of late, several federal commissions have been established to examine the need and potential for reforming the system. More important perhaps has been the resurgence of congressional proposals that range from incremental expansions of existing programs to the establishment of national health insurance. The activities and reactions of the states reflect the federal landscape of proposals, with a wide spectrum of initiatives from rationed care to insurance-based approaches to universal coverage. Finally, the private sector has advocated various reform approaches over the decades, depending on current economic or social forces and perceptions about the nature of private sector involvement. Some of the most significant proposals for reform are discussed in the chapters that follow.

Lessons from Abroad

In searching for answers to America's health care problems, analysts since the 1960s have turned their attention to the United Kingdom, Canada, and more recently to Japan and Germany (see figures A.3 and A.4). These countries offer greater access to health care at seemingly lower costs. These models have become more attractive as the United States continues to make a very poor showing in infant mortality and other indicators of health status.

But also at issue is the image of a democracy that is in a position of denying or helping to deny health services to its citizens in need. In addressing these issues, it is generally acknowledged that America will need to develop a system that incorporates and reflects our unique social values and our cultural and historic heritages.

Quality, Outcomes, and Effectiveness of Care

While concerns about the quality of health care are not new, the emphasis has expanded over the last three decades from a global concern with "quality assurance" to the measurement of effectiveness of specific treatments and the development of practice guidelines for specific medical conditions. Researchers have approached quality through the assessment of the structure of services, the activities of providers and the outcomes of patients. The parameters for measurement and evaluation were identified early in the 1970s by Avedis Donabedian and have been modified and refined since that time.

In earlier decades, quality of care was defined in technical terms. Today, the perspectives of providers, payers, and consumers of health services bear on a variety of investigations that may account in many ways for the changing nature of quality and some of the difficulties in developing measures. These interests also have greater involvement in many decision-making areas of quality of care. For example, patient involvement in quality of care matters was heightened when consumer representatives were included on the boards of Medicare peer review organizations (PROs).

The demand for quality measures has also resulted from the greater availability of data that could perhaps help to define or characterize quality care. These data include information on hospital discharges and, in some states, outpatient procedures. The raw material with which many analysts feel we can measure the performance of the health care system is contained in computerized population-based data files, including Medicare, Medicaid, Blue Cross/Blue Shield, and other third-party payers.

In this regard, the Health Care Financing Administration (HCFA) has been one of the organizations to take the lead in effectiveness initiatives and to promote research on the outcomes of care. The data bases of claims payment and data collected by the PROs have been significant in HCFA's efforts to improve its data banks. The PROs, under contract to Medicare, have sorted thousands of records from that program for several diagnostic categories. Treatment modalities have been compared against outcome measures, including death, readmission, total costs, and post-hospital care, to help develop better quality measures.

During the 1970s, when there was a strong push towards regulation and control of the entire health system, the PROs, and the PSROs before them, played important roles in quality assurance questions in terms of accountability. Today, many question whether the medical profession and health care institutions can be regarded as unbiased and free of self-interest, particularly in light of the competitive nature of the health care environment. Providers have also criticized the federal government, and specifically HCFA, for letting budget concerns dominate the health policy debate, to the seeming detriment of quality of care.

New issues of accountability have emerged that need to be addressed. One such issue relates to standards and standard setting in order to judge the care provided. Physicians in particular have feared that the imposition of federally approved procedures would lead to "cookbook" medicine. There is also considerable interest in the costs of quality assurance activities to health care institutions and some research is under way in this area.

A relatively small proportion of the procedures or services provided to patients has ever been subjected to rigorous evaluation to determine effectiveness or to compare the costs and benefits of alternative treatments. Until now, the federal government limited reviews in this area primarily to a narrow set of considerations regarding safety and efficacy of new drugs and devices.

During the 1980s, findings from leading analysts such as John E. Wennberg, David Eddy, and Robert Brook shed light on the measures and outcome of patient care. Wennberg and others found that variations in the number and type of medical procedures performed was due more to differences in physicians' beliefs about the need for and choice of treatment than to differences in patients' illnesses. Eddy looked at existing evidence of appropriateness, including review of outcomes of alternative treatments for certain surgical procedures. And Brook too contributed new information about the appropriate use of procedures and the use of new technology. These studies helped to create intense concern among policymakers and employers that medical care is not only too expensive but also may be inappropriate in many cases.

Discussions of quality and the value of services have been raised to a new level of sophistication by efforts to measure the patient outcomes of various health care procedures, develop professional guidelines of appropriate use of medical procedures, conduct systematic analyses, streamline administrative and clinical processes, and otherwise enourage health care professionals to practice in ways that yield better outcomes. There is an implicit hope, especially among purchasers, that this focus on outcomes will lead to the ability to control spending increases in the future. Such activities are receiving more federal funding. In addition, an increasing number of congressional mandates call for investigation of these issues.

Finally, employers have showed great interest in this quality revolution; many employers use the lexicon of quality and value to define their health care purchasing practices. Employers want assurances; they want to know that they are getting good value for the dollars spent on health care and continue to participate in the debate about the costs and benefits of health care.

Access to Health Care for Special Populations

Numerous health care programs have been targeted to specific sub-populations with special needs. Yet there remain dramatic needs for care, including long-term care, well-baby and maternity care, nursing home care, home health care, health promotion, disease prevention, substance abuse treatment, and crisis intervention. Despite special attention, mothers and chldren, the poor, elderly, chronically ill, and rural populations continue to require priority attention. At the same time, there is growing recognition that services that benefit the entire community may be in jeopardy in many parts of our country.

The rationale for targeting populations has been the desire to create more equitable health care delivery. Perhaps, targeting best symbolizes the incremental approach to change that has occurred. Some analysts interpret this approach as the most politically pragmatic and practical, if not the most responsible for it extends services by building on existing political and social structures. However, the intricate administrative and bureaucratic mechanisms that accompany programs for targeted populations raise significant concerns about the cost-saving element. Analysts point to the Medicaid program in this regard.

Targeting too may be held up as another indication that the health care system lacks vision and purpose. Some targeting of populations calls into question society's commitment to the needy and under-served as well as the missions of those institutions that serve them. These complex problems are given more detailed consideration in a later chapter.

Rationing Health Care

In contrast to calls to expand services to particular populations, there is frequent mention of rationing of services. New for the 1990s, according to many health care analysts, is the very direct and forthright nature of the dialogue on the issue. Observers agree that rationing has always occurred in the system. Though often in a subtle fashion, care has been limited in terms of access to technology and expensive procedures or entrance to certain hospitals.

Some observers say that what distinguishes the United States from other countries that have universal access is that we ration by denying access to care for a substantial proportion of the population while other countries ration in terms of price controls, technology, and quality.

The call for explicit rationing of services raises medical, legal, and ethical concerns. As evidenced in the articles and commentaries that follow, policymakers of the 1990s will be challenged to consider the implicit or explicit nature of rationing, the controls that will limit access, the populations and levels of care that will be affected, and the impact of sharing scarce or not-so-scarce resources on the American people.

Discussions of rationing have been focused on how to channel our limited health care resources in the direction of greatest individual and social need and benefit. This may mean discouraging what appears to be less beneficial use or overuse by some people and diverting the resources saved to people and services where they are deemed to be of greater benefit.

The rationing debate in many ways epitomizes the dilemma of the last several years. For some, it turns into an argument for structural reform of our system to allow greater equity for our society. For others, it seems to be an effort to try to live a little more reasonably with rising costs and perhaps to even cut costs by eliminating excess. For all, it signals that rising costs have pushed us to acknowledge the limits of what we can afford and to focus on how to use our limited resources better.

Summary

It is clear that key questions arise about access, costs, and quality that will require resolution by the policymakers of the 1990s. Among these questions are the following: (1) Given the state of the American economy and the national deficit, how will the government afford the cost of an array of programs from education to defense, but particularly in health care? (2) Will health care reform proposals aggravate or worsen the problem of rising health care costs in the future? (3) Can we improve the system by continuing a patchwork approach to fix elements of the system or has the time come for a more radical restructuring of the system? (4) What will be the role for private insurance? (5) How can payers and providers collaborate to resolve conflicts and jointly manage costs and the clinical aspects of care? (6) How can society best meet the needs of special populations, including the poor and elderly? (7) Can available funds and services be allocated to meet society's need and demand for health care?

Health Care Statistics

The following figures and tables present significant data on the current health care environment, thus providing greater statistical detail to enhance understanding of the data and policy issues referred to in the abstracts, excerpts, and commentaries that follow.

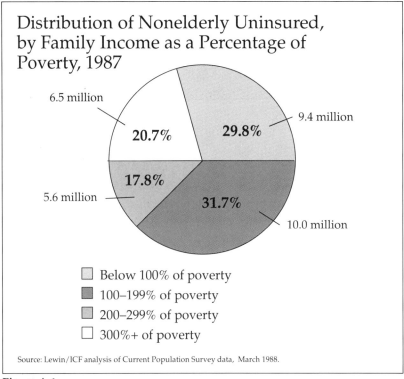

Distribution of Nonelderly Uninsured, by Family Income as a Percentage of Poverty, 1987

- 6.5 million — 20.7%
- 9.4 million — 29.8%
- 5.6 million — 17.8%
- 10.0 million — 31.7%

☐ Below 100% of poverty
■ 100–199% of poverty
▨ 200–299% of poverty
☐ 300%+ of poverty

Source: Lewin/ICF analysis of Current Population Survey data, March 1988.

Figure A.1

Table A.1
Work Force Connections of the Uninsured, 1987
(in millions)

States	Number Uninsured	Percent of Total
Employed persons	14.4	45.7
Full-time workers	11.7	37.1
Part-time workers	2.7	8.5
Nonworking dependents of workers	9.4	29.8
Dependents of full-time workers	7.9	25.1
Dependents of part-time workers	1.5	4.7
Uninsured with no connection to employment	7.7	24.5
Total uninsured	31.5	100.0

Source: Lewin/ICF analysis of the March 1988 Current Population Survey data.

Table A.2
Nonelderly Uninsured Persons, by Age, Sex, and Race/Ethnicity, 1987

	Number of Uninsured Persons (in millions)	Percentage of All Uninsured	Uninsured as Percentage of Persons in Group
Age of individual:			
Less than 18	8.9	28.2	13.2
18-24	6.1	19.4	27.3
25-44	11.4	36.2	14.7
45-64	5.1	16.2	11.2
Sex of individual:			
Male	16.7	53.1	15.8
Female	14.8	46.9	13.8
Race/Ethnicity			
White	24.5	77.8	13.7
Non-white	7.0	22.2	20.3
Hispanic*	6.0	19.0	32.4
All nonelderly persons	31.5	100.0	14.8

* Hispanics are white and non-white.

Source: Lewin/ICF analysis of the March 1988 Current Population Survey data.

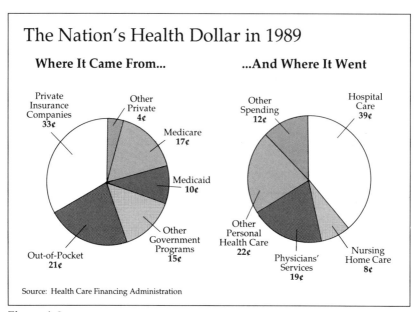

The Nation's Health Dollar in 1989

Where It Came From...   **...And Where It Went**

Private Insurance Companies 33¢

Other Private 4¢

Medicare 17¢

Medicaid 10¢

Other Government Programs 15¢

Out-of-Pocket 21¢

Other Spending 12¢

Hospital Care 39¢

Other Personal Health Care 22¢

Physicians' Services 19¢

Nursing Home Care 8¢

Source: Health Care Financing Administration

Figure A.2

Table A.3

National Health Expenditures, U.S. Population, and Gross National Product: Statistics for Selected Years

NATIONAL HEALTH EXPENDITURES	1965	1975	1985	1989
Total (amount in billions)	$41.6	$132.9	$420.1	$604.1
Private Funds	31.3	77.8	245.0	350.9
Public Funds	10.3	55.1	175.1	253.3
Federal	4.8	36.4	123.6	174.4
State and local	5.5	18.7	51.5	78.8

NATIONAL HEALTH EXPENDITURES AS PERCENTAGE OF TOTAL EXPENDITURES				
Private	75.3%	58.5%	58.3%	58.1%
Public	24.7	41.5	41.7	41.9
Federal	11.6	27.4	29.4	28.9
State and local	13.2	14.1	12.3	13.0

U.S. POPULATION (IN MILLIONS)[1]				
	204.0	224.7	247.0	256.6

PER CAPITA EXPENDITURES				
Total	$204	$592	$1,700	$2,354
Private	154	346	992	1,367
Public	50	245	709	987
Federal	24	162	500	680
State and local	27	83	208	307

GROSS NATIONAL PRODUCT (IN BILLIONS)				
	$705	$1,598	$4,015	$5,201

NATIONAL HEALTH EXPENDITURES AS PERCENTAGE OF GROSS NATIONAL PRODUCT				
	5.9%	8.3%	10.5%	11.6%

AVERAGE ANNUAL RATE OF GROWTH FROM PREVIOUS YEAR SHOWN				
Total health expenditures	8.9%	12.3%	11.0%	11.1%
Private funds	8.9	10.7	11.2	11.1
Public funds	9.1	14.8	10.7	11.0
Federal	10.6	15.5	11.4	11.3
State and local	7.9	13.5	9.2	10.2
U.S. population	1.4	0.9	1.0	0.9
Gross national product	6.5	9.5	8.0	6.7

[1] July 1, 1990 Social Security area population estimates
Note: Numbers and percentages may not add to 100% because of rounding
SOURCE: Health Care Financing Administration, Office of the Actuary: Data from the Office of National Cost Estimates

National Health Expenditures in 1989, by Source of Funds and Type of Expenditure
(Amount in Billions)

	Total All Sources	Private All Private Funds	Government Federal	State Local
National health expenditures	$604.1	$350.9	$174.4	$ 78.8
Health services and supplies	583.5	342.7	164.8	76.1
Personal health care	530.7	315.3	158.4	57.0
Hospital care	232.8	108.3	92.9	31.6
Physicians' services	117.6	78.5	31.8	7.4
Dentists' services	31.4	30.7	0.4	0.3
Other professional services	27.0	21.6	4.1	1.4
Home health care	5.4	1.3	3.1	0.9
Drugs and other medical nondurables	44.6	39.3	2.5	2.8
Vision products and other medical durables	13.5	11.0	2.2	0.3
Nursing home care	47.9	22.7	16.2	9.0
Other personal healthcare	10.5	2.1	5.2	3.3
Program administration and net costs of private health insurance	35.3	27.4	4.3	3.6
Government public health activities	17.5	--	2.1	15.4
Research and construction	20.6	8.2	9.7	2.8
Research	11.0	0.8	8.8	1.4
Construction	9.6	7.4	0.8	1.4

Source: Health Care Financing Administration, Office of the Actuary: Data from the Office of National Cost Estimates

Table A.5

Medicare and Medicaid Data

	1975	1985	1990	% Change 1975-90
Medicare				
Beneficiaries (in millions)	23.8	30.1	33.1	39%
Outlays (in billions)				
Part A	$10.4	$47.8	$65.9	533%
Part B	$3.8	$21.8	$41.5	992%
Total	$14.2	$69.6	107.4	656%
Medicaid				
Beneficiaries (in millions)	22.0	21.8	25.5	16%
Outlays (in billions)	$6.8	$9.3	$41.1	504%

Source: Fiscal 1992 Budget Proposal of the President, February 1991.

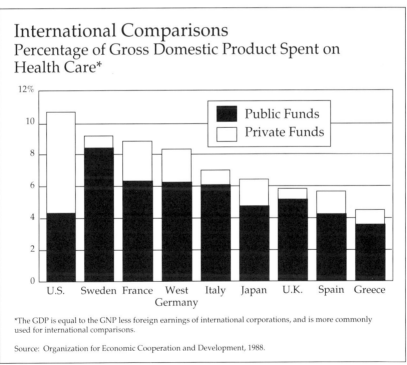

International Comparisons
Percentage of Gross Domestic Product Spent on Health Care*

*The GDP is equal to the GNP less foreign earnings of international corporations, and is more commonly used for international comparisons.

Source: Organization for Economic Cooperation and Development, 1988.

Figure A.3

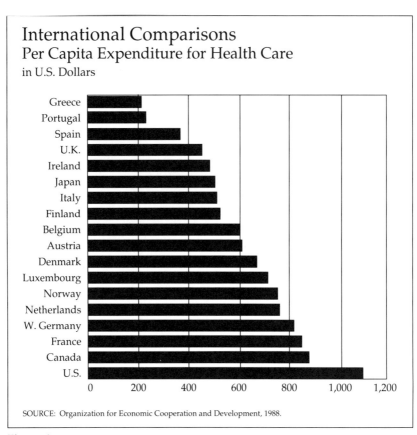

International Comparisons
Per Capita Expenditure for Health Care
in U.S. Dollars

SOURCE: Organization for Economic Cooperation and Development, 1988.

Figure A.4

CHAPTER II

Policymaking for Health Care Delivery

1990 Review and Prospects for 1991

C. Ross Anthony

Considerable uncertainty and flux characterized 1990 as policymakers at both the federal and state levels searched for answers to vexing health care policy issues. The constant balancing of the fundamental health care objectives of cost, access, and quality continues to determine public health policy, much as it has for the past 30 years. Policymakers have reacted by trying to balance the reality of limited resources with a desire to increase access and quality of care. This resulted in continued change in health care policy and an active debate on the future of the health care delivery system.

Federal health care policy continues to be dominated by the national budgetary crisis. Medicare as the fastest growing portion of the domestic budget is coming under special scrutiny at a time when some 31-37 million Americans are without adequate health insurance protection. Because Medicare payments account for the lion's share of the federal health budget, a substantial portion of congressional debate focuses on this program. Policymakers are also turning their attention to research on effectiveness and appropriateness of care in attempts to discover what works best in the practice of medicine. The goals of this work are to improve the quality of care and to limit the use of inappropriate or ineffective treatments.

After examining the health care environment, this paper reviews the major federal and state health care policy issues of 1990 in the context of cost, access, and quality; and then forecasts the likely important issues for 1991. In Medicare, these policy issues include financing, cost-related issues (e.g., hospital payment, physician payment reform, and medical education), issues of efficient program management, access to care (e.g., coverage policy, mammography, prevention), efforts to improve the quality of care (e.g., effectiveness research, PRO review, and clinical research), and major innovations in data systems. In addition to the above issues dealing with incremental change, substantial debate and analysis are focusing on ways to reform our entire health care system. Medicaid expansions also impose new requirements on states to cover low income pregnant women, children, and the elderly while states, in turn, grapple with their own growing fiscal problems.

It should not surprise the reader to discover that many of the articles in this book represent research that either has already been instrumental in shaping the adoption and implementation of policies described here or has laid the intellectual foundation for the policy debates and changes of the future.

Policy Environment

Health care in the United States is shaped and affected by the general environment that sets the stage for all social, economic, and political activities. Certain underlying forces produce changes in the organization and financing of health care and usually come together in the political arena to help determine changes in national health care policy. In 1990, federal health care policy was conducted in a very difficult environment. Budget deficits mushroomed as political fragmentation eroded the power and influence of congressional leaders and the President and the economy slipped towards recession. To some extent all of these events were overshadowed by the crisis in the Middle East and the incredible changes in Eastern Europe and the Soviet Union.

Economic Environment: The Budget and the Economy
Large, continuing federal deficits continued to be the most important determinant of the policy environment. In 1990, the annual effort to meet the Gramm-Rudman-Hollings deficit reduction target became a

national crisis as the Congress and the administration struggled to reach a compromise on tax increases and spending reductions that still left a deficit of $327 billion — some $263 billion over the Gramm-Rudman-Hollings target at the beginning of the year.

Not surprisingly, health care expenditures on Medicare and Medicaid came under close scrutiny during the budget process. While Medicare represents only about 14 percent of federal expenditures, it is the fastest growing portion of the federal budget and one of the few domestic programs of substantial size that is politically available for budget reduction.

In November 1990, President Bush signed into law the Omnibus Reconciliation Act of 1990 (OBRA90), which Congress had passed on 28 October 1990. This legislation reduced projected fiscal 1990 Medicare expenditures by $3.0 billion and increased Medicare related premiums, deductibles, and taxes by $350 million dollars. For fiscal years 1991-1995 the budget package will take $27.9 billion from Medicare providers, $10.1 billion from beneficiaries, $1.9 billion from pharmaceutical companies in Medicaid drug discounts, and will shift some $6.3 billion in costs to private insurers and other companies. In addition, it will raise Medicare payroll taxes by $26.9 billion. Over these next fiscal years, health care's contribution to deficit reduction will be more than $69.2 billion or 14 percent of the proposed $492 billion deficit reduction package.

Any doubt that the deficit would continue to dominate health policy considerations should be dispelled by the Office of Management and Budget's 8 January 1991 reestimate of the size of the deficit. The worsening economy has caused the deficit for fiscal 1991, originally estimated in January 1990 at $105 billion, to grow to $318 billion. The new estimate does not include funds needed for the war in the Middle East and includes the $66 billion surplus in social security this year. Taking these figures into account, the present estimate of the federal government's operating deficit is over $400 billion, out of a total budget of almost $1,400 billion. As the economy slides into recession, the need for services will continue to rise as the government's ability to fund such services falls.

Health Care Environment
The health care environment is characterized by a growing list of critical needs and basic demographic forces likely to exacerbate those problems

in the coming years. It has been estimated that 31-37 million Americans have no health insurance and many millions more are inadequately covered. Cost escalation has created a situation where many private employers no longer feel able to provide health insurance and all payers, including private firms and the government, seek to limit their financial liability and shift the burden of payment to some other payer.

Health care financing problems will be exacerbated by the aging of the population and new diseases like AIDS. In 1950, only 8 percent of Americans were 65 or older. By 2030, some 21 percent will be in that age group. The growth among the oldest old — those 85 and older — is even more rapid. This is an important trend inasmuch as those individuals 85 and older are in greatest need of long-term care services. In 1980 there were 2.2 million in this very old population group, whereas by the year 2030 this group is expected to grow to over 8.6 million.[1]

Political Environment
Reaching a budget compromise in 1990 strained the political process and underscored the political fragmentation that has evolved in this country. The fragmented and diverse views of the electorate are reflected in the congressional and presidential profiles of the last decades; the American people have sent a Republican President and Democratic Congress to Washington 18 of the past 22 years. In addition, members of Congress represent their diverse districts and often defy the congressional leadership as evidenced by the fall 1990 vote against the summit budget compromise reached between congressional leaders and the administration. This political fragmentation has made it difficult for the administration and Congress either to reach consensus on most controversial issues or to pass legislation that proposes major changes to the system. In the absence of a crisis that coalesces opinion or presidential involvement and initiative, it is unlikely that federal policymakers will reach consensus on issues like major health systems reform in the near future.

Finally, health care issues often take a back seat to other pressing domestic and international issues. While the Middle East crisis has dominated congressional attention in recent months, issues such as tax increases, the savings and loan and banking crises, the environment, and the economy all seem to occupy a higher priority on the national agenda at this time than does health care. This situation could change, but it appears that in 1991 health care will not be high on the national agenda.

Medicare Financing Issues

Federal policy that deals with the financing of the Medicare program — the major recipient of federal funds — continues to focus on ways to control costs and to reallocate some funds to finance high priority expansions in Medicare and Medicaid. In general, Congress sought in 1990 to expand prospective payment systems beyond hospitals, reduce expenditures where possible, and shift somewhat the burden of budget reduction away from the inpatient hospital sector towards physician and other medical payments.

Physician Payment

Over the past few years, the government has sought to rationalize its Medicare physician payment system to increase payments for cognitive services while at the same time seeking ways to reduce the rapid increases in physician expenditures. In the Omnibus Budget Reconciliation Act of 1989 (OBRA89) Congress passed a comprehensive physician payment reform plan. The plan, which is one of the most significant changes to the Medicare program since its inception, included four key elements: 1) a fee schedule developed from a resource-based relative value scale (RBRVS), 2) Medicare volume performance standards (MVPS), 3) new limitations on beneficiary liability, and 4) a new program of effectiveness research. The Health Care Financing Administration (HCFA) and the Physician Payment Review Commission (PPRC) spent most of 1990 developing ways to refine and implement the legislation while Congress passed new legislation refining and expanding the reform package.

The new fee schedule is based on the valuation of each physician's service determined by resource inputs. These inputs are work (time and intensity), practice costs, and the liability insurance costs associated with the provision of these services. Relative values so established will then be multiplied by a conversion factor to obtain Medicare payment amounts.

Work on the RBRVS has largely been done under the direction of William Hsiao, Ph.D., at the Harvard School of Public Health. HCFA and the PPRC have spent much of the last two years refining and perfecting this work and moving towards implementing a resource-based relative value determined fee schedule on 1 January 1992. On 4 September 1990 HCFA published a model fee schedule that was required by law and laid out how the agency planned to determine relative values for physician services.

The agency also solicited public comment on a number of issues for which answers have yet to be found. These issues included valuing those services that were not surveyed, identifying services that should be included in the definition of the global bundles for surgical procedures, determining the value of visit services and site-of-service differentials, and estimating physician behavioral reactions to payment changes. Further, the development of final payment rates requires resolution of the appropriate geographic cost of practice adjustment and the development of a budget neutral conversion factor. The calculation of both of these factors is scheduled for completion by fall 1991 and is likely to prove quite controversial.

Limitations on the amount that physicians can balance bill a beneficiary beyond the Medicare reasonable charge went into effect on 1 January 1991. Over three years beginning 1 January 1991, these limits will be phased from 125 percent to 115 percent of the fee schedule amount. Congress relaxed these limits in the first year for evaluation and management services setting the limit for these services for 1991 at only 140 percent — instead of 125 percent — so that a reduction in overall compensation for primary care services will not result before the anticipated increase from the RBRVS fee schedule is implemented in 1992. In spite of this temporary slow down, the changes in beneficiary liability will reduce beneficiary out-of-pocket expenses for balanced billing by 75 percent[2] when the fee schedule is fully implemented.

During 1990, both HCFA and PPRC have made recommendations to the Congress on the Medicare MVPS for fiscal 1991. Congress considered these recommendations after legislating significant reductions in physician expenditures, and laid out a rigid methodology that HCFA should use to set the final MVPS in OBRA90. OBRA90 resulted in final MVPS of 3.3 percent for surgical and 8.6 percent for non-surgical services.

Finally, to reach its budget objectives, Congress is increasingly looking to physician expenditures as a target for reductions. More than $9.6 billion of the $27 billion in provider reductions in OBRA90 came from a reduction in the rate of increase in physician expenditures. This legislation eliminated any update in Medicare fees except for primary care services, again reduced payment for "overvalued procedures," and cut payments for radiology, anesthesiology, and assistants at surgery. In balancing cost and access pressures, only a very few new benefits were funded. These included coverage of mammography screening and injectable drugs for treatment of osteoporosis.

Hospital Payment
In recent years, hospitals have borne the brunt of the government's efforts to reduce the rate of growth of Medicare expenditures. On Capitol Hill, 1990 was characterized by congressional awareness of the deteriorating financial situation of a growing number of hospitals and continued efforts to assist certain classes of hospitals, particularly rural and disproportionate share hospitals. Extension of prospective payment for hospital outpatient services and capital costs is being examined while congressional concerns over access have led to proposals to link nonprofit hospitals' tax exempt status to the amount of charity care provided.

1. *The Prospective Payment System* — Recent studies have indicated that the prospective payment system (PPS) and the racheting down of payment updates by Congress have succeeded dramatically to achieve the objective of reducing the rate of increase in Medicare hospital costs. Three separate studies found that hospital expenditures were reduced by more than one-fifth what they otherwise would have been. A Catholic Health Association study[3] showing that in-hospital payments were reduced by 27 percent in fiscal 1990 was recently confirmed by a Congressional Budget Office (CBO)[4] study that had estimated a 26.9 percent reduction by 1988. The CBO study indicated that while physician expenditures were 100 percent of what they would have been if 1981 trends continued to 1988, hospitals were receiving only 73.9 percent of what they would have otherwise.

As PPS payment increases have lagged behind inflation, a steady erosion of hospital profit margins has resulted. The June 1990 report of the Prospective Payment Assessment Commission (ProPAC) noted that average Medicare hospital operating margins fell to 2.6 percent in PPS5 (FY1989) while the margins for rural and urban hospitals fell to 3.6 percent and -2.3 percent respectively. Projections by ProPAC, HCFA, and the hospital industry all indicate that Medicare operating margins continue to fall.

The deteriorating financial situation of hospitals under Medicare has convinced Congress that much of the industry is at risk. While this has resulted in less severe reductions in the hospital update than in recent years, payment rate increases are still well below the increase in inflation (i.e., the market basket). In OBRA90, Congress set the hospital update as follows: FY1991, market basket minus 2.0 percent; FY1992, market basket minus 1.6 percent; FY1993, market basket minus 1.55 percent; and FY1994-95, market basket.

2. *Rural Health* — Congress continued to be concerned about the financial status of rural facilities. Rural hospitals will receive higher updates than other hospitals to eliminate the differential in small urban and rural standardized payments rates by fiscal 1995. Congress also passed legislation expanding coverage to services provided in community health centers under Medicare, and exempted these facilities and sole community hospitals from reductions in capital payments.

3. *Disproportionate Share* — Congress also chose to increase payments to disproportionate share hospitals. Disproportionate share hospitals are hospitals that have a high percentage of Medicaid and poor Medicare patients. Many are teaching hospitals. The adjustment that a qualifying disproportionate share hospital receives varies depending on its location (i.e., rural/urban) and size, but in all cases the disproportionate share adjustments were increased. This should assist hospitals that serve a large number of poor patients.

4. *Capital and Outpatient Payment* — Prospective payment for both hospital capital and outpatient services received considerable attention in 1990. Congress directed HCFA to develop a proposal for including payments for hospital capital into the prospective payment system by 1 October 1991. The hospital industry has vigorously opposed folding capital into the PPS system, thus setting the stage for heated debate in Congress in 1991.

To reduce the rate of growth of the Medicare program, Congress showed a continuing interest in reforming Medicare payment for outpatient services. In OBRA90, Congress directed the U.S. Secretary of Health and Human Services to develop a proposal by 1 September 1991 for paying for hospital outpatient services under a prospective payment system. However, Congress has not waited for the development of this system before cutting outpatient payments. OBRA90 reduced Medicare payments for outpatient services by 5.8 percent. Medicare payments for outpatient capital would be cut by 15 percent in fiscal 1991 and 10 percent in fiscal years 1992-1995.

5. *Tax Exempt Status* — Policymakers have also begun to carefully

examine and question the tax exempt status of nonprofit hospitals that do not appear to be providing "sufficient" charity care. Until recently, the tax exempt status of nonprofit hospitals, granted by all states, was taken for granted and rarely questioned. The federal tax exemption for nonprofit hospitals can be found in section 501(c)3 of the Internal Revenue Code, which exempts organizations that are "organized and operated exclusively for charitable purposes." Since 1969, the Internal Revenue Service has required that hospitals meet the "community benefits standard" to receive a tax exemption. Hospitals must demonstrate that they are nonprofit, operate in a manner that benefits the community, and offer services to all individuals. The latter is demonstrated by accepting Medicare and Medicaid patients and operating a full-time emergency room.

State and local governments with shrinking tax bases and severe budgetary pressures have attempted to increase revenues by limiting the tax deductibility of nonprofit hospitals. With such actions, these governments are attempting to force nonprofit hospitals to provide their "fair share" of charity care. These efforts that concentrated on seeking to impose property taxes on nonprofit hospitals gathered steam after the Utah Supreme Court upheld a Utah county's levy of taxes on a nonprofit hospital. The rationale for the levy was that the hospital had not demonstrated a clear act of giving and, therefore, was not a charitable institution. Presently, at least 20 state and local governments are questioning the tax exemptions of nonprofit hospitals.

Recent debate at the federal level has focused on whether nonprofit hospitals provide sufficient uncompensated care to deserve a tax deduction. Fueling the debate was the release in May 1990 of *Nonprofit Hospitals: Better Standards Needed for Tax Exemption,* a report by the General Accounting Office (GAO). The GAO concluded that levels of charity care varied greatly among hospitals and suggested that "if Congress wishes to encourage nonprofit hospitals provide charity care to the poor and underserved and other community services, it should consider revising the criteria for tax exemption and reestablish the link between tax exemption and the level of charity care provided by hospitals."

Although hospital groups and some policy experts have severely criticized the GAO report, a number of members of Congress have introduced legislation designed to tie tax exemption for hospitals to the amount of indigent care provided. Representative Edward R. Roybal (D-Calif.) introduced legislation that would require that a nonprofit hospital, unless it can demonstrate financial inability, provide charity care equal to one-half the value of its tax exemption. Representative Brian Donnelly (D-Mass.) in H.R.2207 has sought to amend the Internal Revenue Code to limit the amount of tax exempt bonds that a nonprofit hospital may offer. If a hospital provides insufficient service to low income individuals, the limit would be $150 million. Representative Donnelly and Representative Beryl Anthony (D-Ark.) have also proposed legislation that would require a hospital to operate a full-time emergency room to qualify for tax exemption.

Although none of these legislative proposals was included in OBRA90, congressional concern is expected to intensify. In addition, federal and state interest in the health care needs of the uninsured and the wish to avoid incurring new financial obligations may lead to increased pressures on hospitals to provide more charity care, especially if the economy continues to slide into recession.

Medical Education

The Medicare program continues to be an important source of funding to teaching hospitals for the clinical training of physicians, nurses, and allied health professionals. Although some important changes relating to medical education occurred in 1990, debate in the Congress and the Council on Graduate Medical Education (COGME) centered primarily on adequate Medicare support of medical education, outpatient training, and medical education of minority students.

In 1990, the administration and Congress discussed reductions payments for both direct medical education costs that fund direct costs of training medical residents, nurses, and allied health professionals, and indirect medical education costs that compensate teaching hospitals for inadequate PPS payments that do not take account of factors such as severity of illness. Although the administration and some members of Congress proposed cutting these payments, Congress did not cut payments to graduate medical education in the final analysis.

In 1990, the Congress considered changes to the direct medical education payment that would have given greater weight to medical residencies in primary care. In addition, legislation was passed that expanded Medicare's funding for nursing education that is conducted on hospital premises as long as such education is related to university-affiliated nursing programs. Final regulations to implement legislation passed in 1984 were promulgated, thus providing payment of training in outpatient settings and payment of residents based on a per-resident amount that grows at the rate of inflation instead of on the basis of costs.

The COGME report, *The Financial Status of Teaching Hospitals; The Underrepresentation of Minorities in Medicine,* dealt extensively with issues of the financial status of teaching hospitals and minority medical education. COGME concluded that the financial status of teaching hospitals continued to erode as a result of "high levels of uncompensated and undercompensated care and the failure of third-party payment to keep pace with rapidly rising costs."[5] COGME also found that the minority applicant pool for medical education continued to decrease partly as a result of poor secondary school preparation and the high debt levels that a majority of students incur to complete their medical education. The council recommended making more federal scholarship aid available and working to improve the programs "which improve the size and quality of the minority applicant pool."

Medicare Coverage Policy

The completion of a proposed regulation to explain Medicare's coverage process as well as legislation that provided a modest increase in services covered under Medicare marked the 1990 legislative agenda. The Medicare regulation, under development for more than five years, explained the process by which Medicare decides whether or not to cover new technologies. In general, coverage is decided by local carriers and intermediaries to reflect local practice, but technologies can be referred to HCFA's central office. There, national coverage decisions are made after HCFA receives medical advice from the Public Health Service. For the first time, HCFA has included in its coverage criteria the cost effectiveness of new technology, thus opening the door to rejecting technologies simply on cost.

In OBRA90 the Congress also decided to cover routine biennial mammography screening for female Medicare beneficiaries. This benefit is slated to cost Medicare $1.2 billion over the next five years. This represents a major step by Congress to expand access to coverage of preventive services. Medicare originally was set up to cover acute illness and until recently rarely covered preventive services.

Medical Effectiveness and Quality of Care

To focus increased attention on medical effectiveness, outcomes of care research, and the development of practice guidelines, Congress included provisions in OBRA90 to create the Agency for Health Care Policy and Research (AHCPR). The overall goal was to improve quality of care. A 17-member Advisory Council was selected in August 1990.

By 1 January 1991, the new agency was to develop practice guidelines and medical review criteria for at least three conditions of importance to the Medicare program. After consulting with HCFA, physician organizations, and other interested parties, AHCPR decided to develop guidelines in the following seven areas:

- visual impairment due to cataracts in the aging eye;
- diagnosis and treatment of benign prostatic hyperplasia;
- pain management;
- diagnosis and treatment of depressed outpatients in primary care settings;
- delivery of comprehensive care in sickle cell disease;
- prediction, prevention, and early treatment of pressure sores in adults; and
- urinary incontinence in the adult.

The first three areas targeted for guideline development are cataracts, benign prostatic hypertrophy, and depression.

In addition to guideline development, the new agency will make grants available to investigate the effectiveness of various diagnostic and therapeutic services. AHCPR has already issued grants to four patient outcome research assessment teams to support research on alternative treatments for low back pain, myocardial infarction, cataracts, and prostatic hypertrophy. Such efforts should be aided by a new consolidated Medicare data base, the common working file, which will facilitate analysis of the continuum of care provided to Medicare beneficiaries. The statute also gives AHCPR a number of responsibilities for data gathering. These efforts are aimed at achieving the long-term goal to make more and better data available for outcomes and effectiveness research.

In another quality-related development, the National Practitioner Data Bank became operational in the fall 1990. The data bank stores information about malpractice awards and settlements, and actions taken by hospitals, professional organizations, and other entities to restrict the privileges of physicians and certain other practitioners. Hospitals are expected to query the data bank to obtain information about current and prospective members of their medical staffs.

In March 1990, the Institute of Medicine released a congressionally-mandated report about quality assurance within the Medicare program. The report called for the creation of a Quality Program Advisory Committee (QualPAC), similar to the commissions providing advice to the Congress on Medicare hospital and physician payment issues, along with a 10-year research effort to shift quality assurance efforts from the current case-based peer review model to one based on the analysis of large data sets. To date the report has engendered little congressional interest, but it is likely to prompt a further review of quality assurance activities.

In 1990, a number of other activities continued to focus attention on quality of care. HCFA again publicly released a number of quality related indicators, including hospital mortality data, nursing home performance information, hospital readmission rates. The Joint Commission on Accreditation of Healthcare Organizations (JCAHO) also released its accreditation findings, and Representative Fortney Stark (D-Calif.) introduced legislation to require all physicians, as a condition of Medicare payment, to pass a competency examination at least every seven years.

In summary, 1990 was marked by a great deal of activity related to quality. A large number of activities, including research, data development, and medical guidelines were begun amid high expectations of significant results. The next few years should be filled with increasing activity and policy debates on how best to utilize the information developed along with a number of achievements in this area.

Public Health

A number of events occurred in 1990 in the federal public health arena that were designed to improve quality and access to care. U.S. Health and Human Services Secretary Louis Sullivan, M.D., has taken an active role in promoting public health issues. He has been particularly outspoken on the dangers of tobacco. His department issued a *Guide to Clinical Preventive Services*, the report of the U.S. Preventive Services Task Force, which provides recommendations for clinical practice on more than 100 preventive interventions for the prevention of 60 target conditions.

For the past few years, various parts of the federal government have focused a great deal of energy towards understanding, financing, and seeking a cure for AIDS. Although no cure is in sight, progress has been made on new drugs and vaccinations for AIDS. Although the explosive growth in funding for AIDS research seems to have slowed, funding for services, largely through Medicaid and Medicare, continues to grow, and pressures for rapid action persist. Partly as a result of pressures brought by AIDS activists, the Food and Drug Administration came under intense scrutiny over the past year. Slow approval of drugs and scandals caused by the submission of fabricated generic drug research findings led to a shake up in the agency.

Finally, Titles VII and VIII of the Public Health Service Act, which provides a variety of programs to support health professions education and training, must be reauthorized in 1991. The *Seventh Report to the President and Congress on the Status of Health Personnel*, released in March 1990, documents a decline in applicants to health professions schools as well as a decline in enrollments and graduates. The report may make it more difficult for the Bush administration to continue to argue that a reduced federal role in health professions education is appropriate because past government efforts have been sufficiently successful to obviate continued federal involvement. At present, it is unclear how the reauthorization process will evolve — particularly in the new budget process environment where increases in funding for these discretionary programs will require reductions in other domestic discretionary programs.

Health Systems Reform

National Reform

The presence of 31-37 million uninsured, eroding access for many others, and rapidly increasing costs have led many to conclude that our health delivery system needs major revision. Over the past year discussion, debate, and examination of major health systems reform has occurred with an intensity not seen for many years. As there are many public and private activities under way designed to examine and/or address health system problems, this paper will touch on only a few, and briefly describe some options available to society.

The Bush administration is reviewing issues and options in a number of ways. In his 1990 State of the Union address, the President directed the Secretary of Health and Human Services to examine the health care delivery system. While the President expressed concern about questions of quality, access, and the uninsured, he committed the administration to do something only about the cost of care. The Secretary has established a task force, headed by Under Secretary Constance Horner, to review and report on these issues, with recommendations due in 1991. In addition, the Quadrennial Social Security Advisory Council, appointed by the Secretary, is reviewing Medicare and health systems reform. The Council, headed by Deborah Steelman, was originally scheduled to report by the end of 1990, but it too is now scheduled to complete its work in 1991.

The congressionally mandated United States Bipartisan Commission on Health Care, also called the Pepper Commission, issued its report and recommendations in March 1990. Although the commission was split on many issues, it recommended substantial expansions in health benefits coverage through employment-based plans, health insurance underwriting and rating reforms, Medicaid expansions, and a long-term care program.

More specifically, the commission felt it could most rapidly move towards universal access to health care by a series of incentives and legislative requirements that employers had to meet in the health care arena. The commission recommended that large firms — those with more than 100 employees — be required to provide health coverage for their employees either by purchasing private insurance or by contributing to a new federal health insurance plan. Small firms at first would be encouraged through tax credits/subsidies to purchase health insurance for their employees, but if 80 percent of firms did not purchase insurance for their employees, small firms would be subject to the mandatory requirement of large firms.

A new federal health insurance program would be established for nonworkers, the low income population, and employees from firms who take advantage of this option. Eventually all individuals would be required to obtain coverage from either their employers or the government plan. The commission then turned its attention to long-term care and proposed a plan that would have assured coverage for the first three months of home and community-based care. It also proposed to set the level at which an individual is considered impoverished at $30,000 (excluding homes).

The commission was criticized because it did not propose a method to finance the $64.8 billion in government expenditures necessary to fund the program ($12 billion for acute care and $42.8 billion for long-term care). Instead the commission recommended that three criteria guide the selection of funding policies: (1) taxes should be progressive; (2) revenues should grow fast enough to keep up with benefit growth;

and (3) individuals of all ages should contribute.

In addition to the above, individual legislators, numerous interest groups, and hospital and physician groups continue to develop and advocate health benefit plans that take a variety of approaches. Although all plans differ, they all tend to include combinations of the following generic policy options:

1. *Social Insurance* — Social insurance or national health insurance has been discussed for many years. There continues to be interest in a Canadian type national health insurance among some advocates in this country.

2. *Employer Provided Insurance* — The most popular approach today seems to either mandate or encourage through incentives the provision of health benefits coverage through employer-based, private insurance plans. Some plans such as that proposed by Senator Edward Kennedy (D-Mass.) and Representative Henry Waxman (D-Calif.) would require all employers to offer a minimum package of health benefits to their employees and their dependents. Others would require employers either to offer employees private insurance or to pay a comparable amount to the government to fund a government run and operated insurance scheme. The latter approach is commonly referred to as the "play or pay" approach.

3. *Tax Code Change and Incentives* — Changes in the tax code have been proposed to provide incentives and subsidies for the purchase of health insurance benefits, particularly by small business.

4. *Risk Pools* — Several states have established "risk pools" to help offer insurance protection for the medically uninsurable. Some policymakers have proposed amending current law so that states can require large self-insured employers to help fund such plans.

5. *Health Insurance Reform* — A number of reforms in the private health insurance system have been advocated. These are designed to ensure that employers — notably small employers — have access to private health benefits coverage without regard to medical underwriting. Further, such reforms are aimed at reducing the higher premium and administrative costs of small group policies. Insurance company policies that deny coverage of "pre-existing conditions" have been criticized by many as creating a whole new category of the uninsured in society.

6. *Medicaid Enhancements* — Medicaid is likely to be expanded to increase eligibility, expand coverage, and provide better payment. Most

proposals in this area assign a high priority to expansions to cover pregnant women, infants, and children.

Surveys show that the public, including many businesses, have concluded that fundamental reform is needed in the health system. A key difficulty is that much of the underlying pressure for change comes from current purchasers — business, labor, and federal and state governments — that are interested in lowering the rate of increase in spending. Accomplishing that objective while also expanding access to those currently uncovered requires politically difficult trade-offs and reallocations of resources. No one plan has been able to mobilize the necessary political consensus for change.

State Systems Reform

In 1990, states found themselves with increasing numbers of people who lacked adequate insurance protection. At the same time, these states were experiencing budgetary difficulties without the ability to deficit finance as the federal government is able to do. Recent information indicates that more than 28 states will have revenue shortfalls in 1991.[6] Because Medicaid is one of the largest expenditure items for most states, states have experimented with alternative ways to better cover the uninsured and to reduce expenses; this is often accomplished by seeking to shift the burden of payment to the federal government. State innovation can be divided into four generic approaches: insurance reform, universal coverage, incremental expansions within the existing system, and radical systems change.[7]

1. *Private Insurance Reform* — Since 1986, The Robert Wood Johnson Foundation has sponsored a series of programs "to provide support to state and local entities for the development and implementation of innovative public/private financing and service delivery arrangements designed to improve access to health care for the uninsured." The program has concentrated on seeking ways to reform and restructure the market for private insurance so that more health insurance is available to small businesses, individuals leaving welfare, and the poor. Of the 15 grants that were awarded, 14 were for programs that were developing indemnity or managed care products for small business.

2. *Universal Coverage* — In 1974, Hawaii was the first state to offer comprehensive health insurance to almost everyone by requiring employers to offer health insurance and expanding Medicaid coverage. In the same year, in response to the Hawaii program, the federal govern-

ment passed the Employee Retirement Income Security Act (ERISA). ERISA exempted self-insured employers from state insurance regulation, including state mandated provisions relating to health insurance and the financing of certain insurance premiums. As most large employers self insure, ERISA has been a major barrier to requiring employers to provide health insurance in most states. Only after a long battle was Hawaii's plan upheld on the grounds that it preceded ERISA.

The Hawaii plan has worked fairly well, but over time the need to update the program has run up against ERISA, which precludes changes to the program not in place before the enactment of ERISA. Over the last year, Hawaii has introduced federal legislation to enable it to update its plan and has also sought to make changes to cover the five percent of the population not presently covered. Hawaii has sought to begin a State Health Insurance Plan (SHIP) that would cover families with incomes below 300 percent of the poverty line who are not already covered. The plan, which would emphasize preventive and primary care, would be paid for with state funds, a monthly income-related beneficiary premium, and a small five dollar deductible.

In April 1988, Massachusetts followed Hawaii's lead by enacting legislation, the Health Security Act, designed to ensure access to care for almost everyone. Employers have challenged the requirement that firms with more than six employees pay a 12 percent tax on the first $14,000 of earnings of employees (a maximum of $1,680). Firms can deduct amounts up to $1,680 from their taxes for expenditures made towards providing employee health insurance. This subtle combination of taxes and deductions is designed to comply with ERISA. There was also a .12 percent tax levied on wages up to $14,000 to help purchase health insurance for the uninsured.

The new law changed state's uncompensated care pool for hospitals in Massachusetts by capping hospitals' liability. The law also stated that once the cap was reached the state would bear responsibility for care. Other provisions include coverage to the unemployed who wish to return to work, a student health insurance plan, and a plan to help develop the small business insurance market.

All has not gone well for the plan. Hospitals have brought suit, opposing the manner in which the uncompensated care pool is being run. The new governor's support for a program passed by his predecessor is still not clear. Finally, the state is experiencing a fairly severe economic downturn. Other states such as California are also considering provisions that would approximate universal coverage.

3. *Incrementalism* — Most states have constitutional or other legal provisions that require balanced budgets. In light of growing need and limited resources, many states have sought an incremental approach that slowly but surely expands health care coverage while seeking ways to more efficiently deliver care.

Washington State is an example of an innovative state that has slowly expanded coverage. In 1987, the state passed a law that established a high-risk insurance pool, expanded prenatal care, and offered financial relief to hospitals serving a large proportion of Medicaid and charity patients. In 1988, Washington expanded coverage of those patients with AIDS and in 1989 it established a program to provide services to pregnant women in high-risk groups, including teenagers, and alcohol- and drug-dependent mothers. The key to Washington's efforts is a Basic Health Plan that gives uninsured individuals under age 65 the option of enrolling in capitated managed care plans with premiums and copays based on ability to pay.

4. *Radical Change* — Some states have boldly set out in other directions. The state of Oregon, for example, has approved legislation that would revamp the Medicaid program by having a citizen group rank all 1,600 services and then have the legislature ration coverage in priority order based on the state funds available to fund Medicaid. The state also is expanding access to care to up to 100,000 additional individuals, setting up a situation where more people would be covered but only for "priority" services.

This "rationing" plan has drawn intense criticism from a number of quarters. For example, Congressman Waxman, whose House committee has jurisdiction over Medicaid, does not want to see mandated Medicaid services waived for the poor. The state will require a waiver from the HCFA or legislation in Congress to proceed. Presently, the state is preparing a waiver request. Other states, including Colorado and Michigan, are also examining the Oregon plan.

It should be noted that in a world of limited resources, resources or care are allocated (i.e., rationed) in some way. In America, these distributive decisions are usually made automatically by the market based on price and the ability to pay. On the other hand, health care is allocated in complex ways, taking account of many factors, including insurance coverage, travel distance, waiting, and price. The Oregon plan has engendered controversy and lively discussion partly because it explicitly deals with the allocation question for the poor and in doing so exposes the fact that not all Americans have access to the same amount or quality of care.

The Oregon plan has succeeded in stimulating intense public debate, which was one of its goals. Nevertheless, the state has also succeeded in revamping the small business health insurance market. The state gives tax credits to small businesses to provide health insurance and has set up a group insurance pool for small businesses. If employers do not take advantage of the incentives in place, the law calls for employers who do not provide insurance by 1994 to pay a tax that will be used to finance health insurance for their employees.

In summary, some states do not feel that they can wait for federal health systems reform. Almost all states are taking innovative steps to offer access to health care to those inadequately insured while seeking new ways to limit and control costs. Much as it has in the past, state innovation is likely to continue and form the basis of any eventual federal action.

Medicaid

Last year, Congress pared $2.9 billion from the federal contribution to Medicaid. About two-thirds of this reduction came by reducing Medicaid payments to makers of prescription drugs and the other one-third by shifting responsibility for some Medicaid patients to private group health plans. These reductions were accompanied by a number of eligibility and benefit expansions.

In the past few years, both the administration and Congress have expressed a desire to better cover pregnant women and children in the Medicaid program. Last year, Congress increased coverage for pregnant women by requiring that states offer Medicaid coverage for services related to pregnancy for women with incomes up to 133 percent of the federal poverty level as of 1 April 1990. States have the option to provide coverage for pregnant women and infants with incomes at or below 185 percent of the federal poverty level.

OBRA90 took steps to expand mandatory coverage for poor children from the present limit of seven years of age to age 18. This expansion is phased in over 10 years in such a way that children age seven or below (children born on or after 30 September 1983) will continually be covered thus expanding coverage by one year per year.

In addition to expanding coverage for poor children, Congress in

OBRA90 required that states pay all Medicare premiums and deductibles for seniors with incomes below 100 percent of the poverty line. In 1993 and 1995, states will be required to cover Medicare premiums and deductibles for seniors with incomes below 110 percent and 125 percent respectively. In addition to expanding financial protection for dually eligible Medicare and Medicaid beneficiaries, Congress expanded options for states to provide home and community-based care to the poor, frail elderly. Congress also protected the ability of states to count "voluntary" contributions towards their required matching of federal funds.

The government has also taken major steps over the past year to improve the quality of care in nursing homes. As a result of an earlier study by the Institute of Medicine, Congress passed legislation in 1989 that fundamentally changed the requirements for treatment and quality enforcement for nursing homes. Over the past two years, HCFA has been working with nursing homes, senior citizen representatives, and the Congress to publish regulations implementing these far-reaching requirements. In 1990, final regulations were published that guarantee nursing home residents basic personal rights, set higher standards of medical care including 24-hour nursing care, and lay out requirements for medical assessment, including mental health assessment and plans of treatment. The law also requires that states increase payments to nursing homes to account for the increased costs of these requirements. Many states have had difficulty implementing these requirements and in some cases (e.g., California, New York) refused to do so until ordered to comply by the courts.

Finally, legislation guaranteeing freedom from bias in employment, public facilities, transportation and communications was passed by Congress. The Americans with Disabilities Act includes protection for HIV-infected persons and those with AIDS.

Next Steps

In 1991, we are likely to see a continuing collision of needs and desires for access to health care and continued pressures due to the constraints of limited resources. Contributing to a battle of forces that may exceed what has been seen for some time are a recession, unemployment, insurance practices, state deficit induced reductions in Medicaid eligibility, and business retrenchment from the provision of health insurance coverage. All these factors are increasing the numbers of uninsured at a rapid rate. This mushrooming need for health care access will clash head on with a strained private economy, growing federal and state deficits, and the new federal budget process which requires pay-as-you-go funding.

The Budget Enforcement Act of 1990, which was part of OBRA90, adjusted Gramm-Rudman-Hollings targets and created a number of other mechanisms that the Congress felt would be effective in controlling the escalating federal debt. Discretionary funds have been divided into three categories for fiscal 1991-1995: defense; domestic; and international. Increases in these categories are required to be budget neutral or paid for by tax increases. Entitlement programs are subject to "pay-as-you-go" rules, which require that any new programs that have budgetary effects over the next five years be paid for by reductions in other entitlement programs or increases in taxes.

The new mechanisms will significantly alter the legislative process that relates to health care programs. As the Medicare program is one of the largest programs usually available for cuts, many have theorized that Medicare will become the "bank" that other programs look to for reductions to fund their expansions. On the other hand, any expansion of health care research at the National Institutes of Health or AHCPR will have to be funded by either reductions in other discretionary programs or a tax increase.

In the final analysis, very little major change is likely to occur in the near term, even though the numbers of uninsured are likely to swell and lively debate is likely to result from congressional hearings and the release of various reports on the national health care system. Instead, Congress and the administration will be fully occupied with implementing and refining the new resource based relative value fee schedule for physician services, planning and implementing major outcomes research and guideline development, and expanding the prospective payment programs to hospital capital payments and outpatient services. The more significant health system reform debate is likely to evolve in 1992 — a presidential election year.

Whereas this will likely be a year of little new legislation, it is equally likely to be a period of active research and publication of new analyses on how to provide better care at reasonable costs. Research on health care financing, alternative delivery systems, medical education, human resources development, and disease prevention will hopefully flower over the coming year, providing policymakers with the vision they need for change when the resources become available.

NOTES

1. U.S. Senate Special Committee on Aging: Aging America: Trends and Projections. Washington, D.C.: Public Health Service, Department of Health and Human Services; 1988.
2. Physician Payment Review Commission. Annual Report to Congress. Washington, D.C.: Physician Payment Review Commission; 1990.
3. Catholic Health Association. Medicare budget actions, implications for hospitals. Washington, D.C.: Health Policy Alternatives; 1989.
4. U.S. Congressional Budget Office. Memorandum to health staff, estimated impact of legislation from 1981 through 1989 on Medicare disbursements. Washington, D.C.: June 27, 1990.
5. Council on Graduate Medical Education. The financial status of teaching hospitals: the underrepresentation of minorities in medicine. Washington, D.C.: U.S. Dept. of Health and Human Services; 1990.
6. *Health Week News*, January 14, 1991.
7. Three of these terms are used in Demkovich L. The states and the uninsured: slowly but surely, filling the gaps. Washington, D.C.: National Health Policy Forum; 1990.

CHAPTER III

Economic Indicators of Health Care Problems

ABSTRACTS AND EXCERPTS

Fuchs VR. The health sector's share of the gross national product. *Science*. 1990;247:534-538.

There is ...widespread concern that the "spurt" of health care has continued for more than 40 years and shows little sign of abatement. Moreover, because the health sector is so large in absolute terms (about $600 billion in 1989), its rapid growth has a particularly traumatic effect on other sectors that compete with it for private and public spending.

Apart from measurement error, the more rapid increase of health care prices can have only two possible explanations: (i) the prices of inputs into health care (that is, labor, capital, intermediate goods, and services) have increased more rapidly than input prices in other sectors, or (ii) productivity in health care has increased less rapidly than in other sectors.

The rapid changes in financing and marketing of health care in recent years may also have contributed to poor productivity performance. Physicians and hospitals now face a bewildering array of insurance plans and they presumably require substantial numbers of clerical personnel to handle the large volume of paperwork. Also, as hospitals and physicians have tried to adapt to the so-called "competition revolution" of the 1980s, there has been a considerable increase in resources going into marketing, advertising, new computer systems, management consulting, and the like.

The possible explanations for the trends in relative quantities of output are more numerous and their interrelationships more complex than for relative prices. The variables that have been mentioned most frequently to explain why use of health care has grown faster than that of other goods and services include "defensive medicine," the aging of the population, new technologies, and the rise of "third party" payment.

More enduring constraints on quantity are likely to emerge from the supply side rather than from demand. The debate over whether or not to ration care is largely irrelevant; the important questions are: Who will ration? Who will be rationed? What will be rationed? There are likely to be attempts to hold down the growth in number of physicians, to limit expansion of medical care facilities and equipment, and to monitor closely the pace and character of technologic innovation. One can only hope that these attempts will be guided by rational analysis, compassion, and an appreciation for the long-run as well as short-run aspects of this complex problem.

Reinhardt UE. Health care spending and American competitiveness. *Health Aff.* 1989;8:5-21.

Reprinted with permission of *Health Affairs.*

The belief that increases in health care costs translate themselves directly into higher product prices seems to be a commonplace in the American business community. It supports the argument that employer-paid health care for active and retired employees renders American producers "noncompetitive" in the global marketplace. Thus have health care costs slipped onto the agenda of thinkers who worry about this nation's future place in the world economy.

First, it is unlikely that high health care costs per se render American business noncompetitive at home or abroad. Second, it is just as unlikely that the relatively large percentage of the American gross national product (GNP) devoted to health care, by itself, adversely affects the nation's competitiveness. Third, if high health care expenditures do affect this nation's international competitiveness, they are likely to do so through the following combination of circumstances: (1) over 40 percent of health care is now being financed through public budgets; (2) American taxpayers and their political representatives want to keep the percentage of GNP going through public budgets constant; which means that (3) public funds spent on health care may well come at the expense of our investment in human capital (education) and the nation's infrastructure, both of which are largely publicly financed.

The last factor is likely to be the most important direct link between our high health care expenditures and our competitiveness.

Even if every increase in the cost of employer-paid health care benefits could immediately be financed by the firm with commensurate reductions in the cash compensation of its employees—so that "competitiveness" in the firm's product market is not impaired—it would leave employees worse off unless the added health spending bestowed upon employees is valued at least as highly as the cash wages they would forgo to finance these benefits. Because it is the perceived value of a firm's compensation package that lures workers to the firm and away from competing opportunities, the typical business firm has every economic incentive to maximize this perceived value per dollar of health care expenditure debited to the firm's payroll expense account. Therein, and not in "competitiveness" on the product side, lies the most powerful rationale for vigorous health care cost containment on the part of the American business community.

COMMENTARY

J. Richard Gaintner

ost now drives the health care systems and will continue to do so for the foreseeable future, at least into the 21st century. Victor Fuchs in his article, *The Health Sector's Share of the Gross National Product*, spells out the details of this trend from 1947 to 1987. He points out that both price and quantity determine cost, and discusses how each of these has affected the cost escalation of health care during that period, from under five percent to more than 11 percent of the gross national product (GNP).

Fuchs goes on to relate price increases to more inputs, especially labor and technology, and lack of improved productivity, which may relate to more regulation, defensive medicine in the litigious environment, more marketing efforts and other factors. Quantity or volume increases result from many factors, including more elderly and chronically ill people, more technologies available, and the buffering effect of third-party payment. He predicts increasing nursing costs and more pressure on physician payments.

In an excellent recent publication from the National Committee for Quality Health Care entitled *Critical Choices: Confronting the Cost of American Health Care*, authors Jack Meyer, Sharon Silow Carroll and Sean Sullivan of New Directions for Policy lay out in considerable detail the complexity and multiplicity of factors driving the cost spiral. They include the following:

1) Demographic trends, especially the aging of the population;
2) Large economic trends, including general inflation and the increase in real personal income;
3) Public health trends, such as the AIDS epidemic, increasing substance abuse and other life-style factors;
4) Insurance coverage trends, including expansion of covered services, more managed care programs, and cost sharing (and shifting!);
5) Government policies such as tax rules, mandated benefits, insurance and other regulations, Medicaid, Medicare, and state programs;
6) New technologies and greater use of existing ones; and
7) The legal system with burgeoning malpractice claims and resultant defensive medicine.

Another factor that might be included is high-profit margins for some medical products and pharmaceutical, especially single-vendor items. I have sometimes gently chided my friends in the for-profit health care product industries for screaming so loudly about their escalating employee benefit costs while at the same time booking sharply rising profits for many items sold to health care providers.

Very high administrative costs in the insurance industry may also be a significant part of the problem. The report *Premiums Without Benefit: Waste and Inefficiency in the Commercial Health Insurance Industry* noted: that "for ever dollar the commercial insurance industry paid in claims in 1988, the industry spent 33.5 cents for administration, marketing, and other overhead expenses....not including profits." Blue Cross/Blue Shield data were not available, the report stated.

Reinhardt discusses health care spending and American competitiveness. In addition to discussing the role of business related to the problems under consideration, especially whether or not health care costs are in fact such a big problem for American companies in a global economy, he raises the spectra of post-retirement medical benefits and their effect on corporate financial health.

Having just gone through extensive consideration of this matter in my own organization, I suggest everyone running a business big or small, health care or not, take a hard look at this issue. A strong case is made for relying on contribution plans rather than defined benefit programs under current and foreseeable economic circumstances.

The emphasis on cost as the major health system problem will continue to have a profound effect on academic health centers and teaching hospitals as they are businesses and health care organizations in addition to educational and research institutions. I believe our institutions must move beyond focusing just on doing biomedical research, science education and service provision, especially super high tech services, and demonstrate leadership in bringing value to the health system.

Leo Henikoff, M.D., president and chief executive officer of Rush-Presbyterian St. Luke's Medical Center in Chicago, set down a simple equation at a retreat of the Board of Directors of the Association of Academic Health Centers several years ago that has profoundly influenced my thinking, and I suggest should do the same for others. He reminded us of the following relationship:

$$V = Q/C \times E$$

in which V = value, Q = quality (science and art), E = efficacy (should the test or operation be done at all?!), and C = cost. He especially noted that if E = 0, then the value is also zero.

We as leaders of academic health centers and hospitals should show the way, not just in the science of medicine but in how to bring value to medicine. We must emphasize quality and efficacy at reasonable cost. Perhaps we could even talk about what not to do; about mortality; about individual freedom vs. the common good (à la Daniel Callahan)[3]; about respect for patient and family values and desires; and about better organization of the health care system, especially how academic centers and community hospitals should work more in collaboration and why we need specialists cooperating with primary care physicians in the most cost-effective ways. Finally, maybe we should demonstrate better leadership in how to care for patients with diseases, not just how to treat diseases in patients. We need to balance science, education, and caring with business, politics, and economics!

As academic health centers pass through the 1990s and enter the next century, hopefully we can lead the way in solving what is far and away the greatest problem we face in our field, and that is the continuing escalation of the cost of health care. Whether health costs go to 15 percent or 20 percent of the GNP as many predict, let us vigorously attack these issues as we have attacked AIDS and the human genome project and find solutions to these most perplexing problems.

REFERENCES

1. New Directions for Policy. *Critical Choices: Confronting the Cost of American Health Care.* Washington, D.C.; Committee for Quality Health Care, 1990.
2. Citizens Fund. *Premiums Without Benefit: Waste and Inefficiency in the Commercial Health Insurance Industry.* Washington, D.C.: Citizens Fund, 1990.
3. Callahan D. *What Kind of Life: The Limits of Medical Progress.* New York: Simon and Shuster, 1990.

W. Douglas Skelton

For those of us involved in organizations which deliver health care and/or health education, the issue of cost of health care is a constant concern.   It serves as the basis, at times innocently and at other times, not so innocently, for many of the negative views of our schools, universities, and academic health centers. The reasons health care expenditures have grown faster than expenditures for other goods and services and accounted for an increasing percentage of the gross national product are complex and not completely understood. Unfortunately, this situation promotes attacks on the health care system or components of the system. In addition, within the system the situation may lead to one part blaming another for increased costs.

Increased wages, lack of productivity gains, defensive medicine, the aging of the population, and the increase in third-party reimbursements have contributed to increased health care costs. Our move to high-technology medicine is cited by many as a cost-enhancing factor, yet it can be and has been cost-decreasing. As Fuchs and Reinhardt demonstrate even these apparently straightforward factors are subject to various interpretations.

In my own state of Georgia, deliberations of a recently completed Access to Care Commission focused on many of these issues. It was most interesting, and somewhat frightening, to see representatives from the insurance industry and other businesses jointly argue that the cost of health care was making Georgia businesses noncompetitive. To see these two groups combine again to support legislation that would allow preferred provider organizations in Georgia to replace financial incentives for a patient to stay within a plan with financial penalties if the patient goes outside the plan further illustrates how tough the fight has become. I expect Georgia is not the only state where the insurance industry will protect their unusually high share of the health care dollar by joining forces with others to blame the physicians and other providers.

Academic health centers vary greatly in terms of their mix of health professional schools, hospitals and clinics, and research programs. The responses of academic health centers to the economic issues in health care vary as well. Central to all actions is a need to keep the medical education issue foremost and to protect the patient and financial bases on which it depends. For Mercer this has meant support for the major affiliated hospital in its goal to remain the provider of choice for patients and for community physicians. This fits nicely with Mercer's development as a community-based medical school with a focus on educating physicians to meet the state's needs for primary care providers in rural or other underserved areas.

Specifically, as a growing medical school our need for specialty physicians for education purposes complemented the hospital's growth as a regional center. Our principal focus on primary care has resulted in the development of an ambulatory center designed to improve the primary care patient base and provide education in the ambulatory setting. Obviously, the analysis preceding such a development included community need and payment availability.

Dollar issues have become a daily aspect of our work in the clinical setting. The principal negative result has been the closure of a needed, but money-losing, clinic in a rural county. On the positive side are the developments referred to above, a decrease in the inpatient length of stay, and a recognition of the hospital as the lowest cost hospital provider in the area—a rarity for teaching hospitals. These are but minor accomplishments in dealing with economic pressures that continue to build. They are not possible for all academic health centers, especially in those centers where the patient mix involves a high percentage of uninsured, Medicare, and Medicaid patients.

Cutbacks in the adequacy of funding for governmental health care programs, that is Medicare and Medicaid, coupled with reductions in Medicare education funding and decreased research support are forcing increased reliance on patient care income to support medical education. As these actions occur counter pressure to "do something" about health care costs continues to build with, as yet, no consensus in sight. It is a Hobson's choice for academic health centers.

CHAPTER IV

Public Dissatisfaction with Health Care

ABSTRACTS AND EXCERPTS

Blendon RJ, Donelan K. The public and the emerging debate over national health insurance. *N Engl J Med.* 1990;323:208-212.

Reprinted with permission of *The New England Journal of Medicine.*

Our review suggests that despite the high level of public interest in a national health care plan, Americans may be unable to agree on a specific proposal, as they were in the 1970s. To build a consensus around a single program that takes into account the attitudes we have described, we propose that five principles be incorporated into proposals for a national health plan.

Principle 1: Any new proposal for universal health care should not try to resolve the dispute over whether the system of financing health care adopted should be predominantly public or predominantly private. Rather, it should contain elements of both.

Principle 2: Any new program of universal health care should rely on taxes other than the progressive income tax for its chief financing.

Principle 3: Some of the resources for a program of universal health care should come from the reallocation of funds already being spent within the health sector or in other (non-health-related) government programs.

Principle 4: So that low-income groups not covered by other universal insurance proposals will be best served, the administration of Medicaid should be transferred to a locus outside the welfare system.

Principle 5: Any new program should be phased in over a period of years.

Ginzberg E. Health care reform—why so slow? *N Engl J Med.* 1990;322:1464-1465.

Reprinted with permission of *The New England Journal of Medicine.*

It is no mystery that major health reforms addressing cost containment and coverage for the uninsured have been so slow in coming. The dominant interest groups—government, employers, and households—as well as the major providers—physicians and hospitals—have reached no agreement on how to change the existing system to accomplish these widely desired reforms. In the absence of a strategy that can command broad support from disparate groups, a political consensus for major reforms will remain elusive. The only reasonable assessment at the beginning of the 1990s is that we are unwilling to risk the strengths of our existing health care system in a radical effort to remedy admittedly serious deficiencies. The American public, in its political inaction, has so far opted for continued temporizing.

Levey S, Hill J. National health insurance—the triumph of equivocation. *N Engl J Med.* 1989;321:1750-1753.

Reprinted with permission of *The New England Journal of Medicine.*

"For the first time ever, national health insurance has a serious chance of passing the Senate during this Congress." So began an article in *The Wall Street Journal* on July 16, 1979.

So astronomical have health costs become, so disappointing the so-called competitive approach to cost control, and so unacceptable the plight of the estimated 37 million Americans who lack insurance (not to mention the millions who are underinsured) that interest has been building again in a new national policy for the financing of health care.

Joining the swelling numbers of those interested in a federally sponsored program of universal health care are prominent political leaders, academics, and providers. Perhaps most surprising is the presence among them of leaders of business and industry. Having recognized the private sector's inability to control inflation in health costs, they are beginning to close ranks behind a national approach. To auto makers and other major manufacturers the approach offers a further possibility of holding down production costs and thus competing successfully in world markets.

We conclude that the historical pattern of equivocation is likely to prevail, because of the power of special-interest groups in American life, the failure to agree on a workable solution, the weakness of resolve of our political leaders, and the lack of widespread discontent in the general population.

In the United States, the federal government has traditionally been the agency of last resort, the final party to intervene on behalf of the public interest. For the protection of our health care system to be extended, either an upwelling of popular discontent or strong, active leadership is necessary. Without such ferment and leadership, the best we can hope for in the direction of universal health care is a series of half measures and fragmented financing mechanisms—more equivocation. We can also expect a familiar refrain: until adequate means are found to close the gaps that allow millions of Americans to go uninsured, we will continue to hear the intermittent call for national health insurance.

COMMENTARY

Ronald P. Kaufman

Included in this section are articles by Robert Blendon, Eli Ginzberg, and Samuel Levey and his colleagues. Despite the diverse background of the authors, all three articles in general seem to reflect a similar theme, that is, increasing discontent with the current health care delivery system of the United States and yet a lack of will to initiate major reform.

With a unique perspective, Eli Ginzberg reviews briefly the varied actions taken over the past 20 years to address health care in the United States. He then asks the question, "How can one explain the apparent contradiction between the public's concern over issues of cost and disenfranchisement and the concomitant absence of successful reform?" Returning again to the historic perspective, he states that it is traditional for the United States to favor more modest approaches rather than major interventions; that the United States is, at least for the moment, still wedded to a pluralistic system; inherent fears of any implication that reform might lead to rationing; and finally, the basic concern of extending government jurisdiction into the arena of health. Dr. Ginzberg's conclusion is that until a coalition of the dominant interest groups can come together, a major change will not occur.

This sentiment is echoed by Levey and his colleagues, with a little more exposition on the issues of the political power of special interest groups, especially the insurance industry and organized medicine, along with a major concern of the public relative to any new taxes, a concern relative to rationing and queuing for important services, and a belief that all of the new proposals on the table are seriously flawed in some critical area. They conclude with the view that Americans lack a necessary level of discontent that would allow the federal government to become the agency of last resort to address this critical societal issue.

Robert Blendon, on the other hand, analyzing survey data, also believes that there is a strong level of support for some form of a national health care program. However, on balance, there is also concern about other major societal issues and perhaps more importantly, major negative feelings and ambivalence about freedom of choice, rationing/queuing, and increasing taxes to support any ambitious program. Therefore, he believes that there will be significant public resistance to any substantive change, since there is no agreement on a specific proposal. He suggests that any proposal must incorporate at least five principles: a combination of a public and private cooperation; raising the dollars necessary to achieve this goal through a "sin" tax approach; assurances that there will be a decrease in the administrative costs; remove Medicaid from the welfare system; and deliberately phasing in the changes, thereby not making them as dramatic as some of the current proposals suggest.

To this reviewer it was surprising that all three authors, despite their diverse backgrounds, analyze the issue essentially identically, that is, there exists a significant level of public discontent relative to the continued escalation of health care costs and concomitantly a significantly increasing number of individuals being disenfranchised through the lack of insurance coverage. The authors also note the significant ambivalence of the American public as to what to do about it and when. This reviewer shares the frustration that underlies these four articles.

A societal problem as significant as access to high quality health care in an era when health care can, indeed, increase the quality of life is distressing for a country as affluent as ours. The lack of political will to address such a problem, although not surprising in a nation as diverse as ours, is nonetheless disappointing. Although the authors all make suggestions on how to address the issue in incremental steps, one cannot help but wonder if the result might not be too little too late. The future of biomedical science and its ability to positively impact the human condition is almost unlimited with much of the potential available today. If we do not address the problems in the near term, we will be burdened not only with increasing costs and more and more people without access, but also we will find ourselves without the ability to apply the new science to the citizens of this nation.

The challenge is how to generate a broad, sweeping consensus for major reform so that the issue can become the focus of debate during the next presidential election. Not to aspire to that goal would be a disservice to society in the most critical area of our social fabric—the health and well being of our citizens.

COMMENTARY

Paul E. Stanton, Jr.

As the cost of our nation's health care continues to rise in astronomical proportions, experts say a viable solution is contingent on public opinion. Despite the efforts in the past two decades by the private as well as the public sectors to curtail health care costs, the nation's expenditures on health care is expected to reach $1.9 trillion by the year 2000. Equally disheartening is the reality that approximately 31-37 million Americans lack health insurance.

In the past, the federal government implemented prospective reimbursement for Medicare and increased subsidies for growth of health maintenance organizations (HMOs). Some states tried to limit spending for Medicaid by allowing very low fee levels for physicians who treated Medicaid patients, and several have adopted certificate-of-need regulations for nursing homes.

In addition, private employers have restructured health insurance benefits and encouraged enrollment in HMOs and preferred provider organizations. However, the dilemma remains prevalent and, once again, the plea for a government-sponsored health care program, patterned after those found in Canada and Great Britain, has become a national issue.

Recent surveys show that political leaders, leaders in business and industry, academics and providers have all joined the ranks for lower health care costs. However, the reality of federal intervention appears to be less desirable to the majority of Americans for several reasons.

While approximately 72 percent of our nation's population say they favor a national program, they in turn rank the increase in health care costs lower than other national issues such as inflation, unemployment, and drug abuse. Other health issues such as the acquired immunodeficiency syndrome and the fear of malpractice have also averted the public's attention.

In addition, studies show that while most Americans favor a national program, they are hesitant to give up their choice of physician or wait longer to receive treatment. The majority of the population also opposes a tax increase to fund a national program as well as a restraint on the amount of money that flows into new technology and innovation. Traditionally, our society has favored slow and minimal government intervention.

Therefore, an obvious contradiction exists in a public that cries for lower health care costs but is hesitant to change the way it receives care. In addition, some analysts say Congress appears less inclined to act decisively on legislation due to the strength of special-interest groups.

However, in some areas of the country, academic health centers are able to help counteract the high cost of medical care by producing primary care physicians. East Tennessee State University's James H. Quillen College of Medicine in Johnson City, Tennessee, was created in order to supply family practice physicians to underserved areas. Primary care clinics can serve approximately 90 percent of the patients treated without seeking additional care from a subspecialist.

For instance, the Quillen College of Medicine opened a Family Health Center in Mountain City, Tennessee (Johnson County) which provides primary care to the rural community. The hospital was closed a few years ago due to lack of funds. This clinic is one attempt to serve the citizens with immediate primary care.

In addition, the university's School of Nursing operates an extended hours clinic in Mountain City in order to provide basic care after clinic hours and on weekends. The school also operates a Homeless Clinic in Johnson City, which provides primary care to the community. The clinic is funded through grants and donations and is considered a responsibility of all participants.

In the near future, the College of Medicine anticipates opening additional primary care clinics that will also serve rural areas and ease a part of the high cost of medical care.

However, the possibility of curtailing high medical costs while continuing to invest in research and technology will remain a problem. In a free society that is burdened with fatal diseases, financial crises, fear of war, and drug abuse, a systematic change in the delivery of medical care may not be in the near future.

CHAPTER V

Proposals to Reform the Health Care Delivery System

American College of Physicians. Access to health care.
Ann of Int Med. **1990;112:641-661.**

Reprinted with permission from the American College of Physicians.

The American College of Physicians believes that there is an increasingly urgent need to address a growing national problem, that of many Americans lacking access to health care. Spiraling increases in health care costs are reducing access to health services, especially for those without health insurance protection or the financial means to pay. Cost containment actions are increasingly undermining the basic infrastructure on which delivery of services depends—facilities and personnel. Further, many of these cost containment actions are eroding the ability of physicians to provide optimum care for their patients.

Having reviewed the major alternative types of proposals for financing access to health care services for all Americans, the College concludes as follows:

A nationwide program is needed to assure access to health care for all Americans, and we recommend that such a program be adopted as a policy goal for the nation. The College believes that health insurance coverage for all persons is needed to minimize financial barriers and assure access to appropriate health care services.

Assuring access also involves issues of cost and quality. The medical profession bears responsibility to ensure that acceptable, appropriate, and cost-effective care is delivered.

A comprehensive and coordinated program to assure access on a nationwide basis is essential. In the near term, given the urgency of the need, it should build on the strengths of existing health care financing mechanisms. In the longer term, careful consideration of new and innovative alternatives, including some form of a nationwide financing mechanism, will be necessary.

Expansion of Medicaid and mandated employer health insurance require immediate consideration for bringing prompt relief to a large segment of the population presently without adequate access to health care. Although these short-term approaches have serious negative implications for achieving long-term reform, they would bring an immediate amelioration of intolerable conditions.

The entire structure of the American health care delivery system must be carefully examined. Alternative approaches for achieving greater access to health care services must be carefully considered, including the possibility of a unified insurance mechanism. The staggering administrative burden of the present system, both in the obvious expense of its administration and in the rising bureaucracy and paperwork that it engenders, drives us towards this conclusion.

Therefore, we urge extreme caution in merely building on the present structure. Although this approach has appeal for various political and practical reasons, we will continue to argue that some proposed solutions should be considered short-term remedies and that the time has come for a thoughtful re-examination of all aspects of the present health care system.

Butler S, Haislmaier E, eds. A national health system for America. Washington D.C.: Heritage Foundation; 1989.

Because of its fundamental flaws, the gaps in the existing health care system can never be closed at acceptable cost without structural changes. To design the necessary reforms, policy makers first must appreciate how the current system originated, and they must understand the economic and political forces that are a product of that historical development.

...today's basic system evolved not in response to the needs of consumers, but according to the marketing and professional objectives of suppliers of health care. This has led to a distorted system of private insurance that provides generous routine coverage, yet little protection for catastrophic costs, and public sector programs that until recently have been virtually an open cash register for the health care industry. The results of such a system could have been predicted: health care costs in recent years have been rising twice as fast as general inflation. Reinforced by perverse incentives in the tax code, these basic features have produced a system that is saturated with both inflationary pressures and glaring gaps in coverage.

Mandating employers to provide coverage, for instance, would force business to shoulder the system's inflationary pressures, triggering an escalation in payroll costs that would lead to cost-saving worker layoffs. Similarly, piling on new Medicare programs without structural reform would further weaken the finances of the program, threatening huge tax increases or eventual reductions in benefits.

Nor does the answer lie in trying to curb price rises through price controls and regulations.

Major reform proposals in recent years exhibit two broad defects. Either they ignore the structural flaws of the current system and advocate major expansions of government activity, or they urge a radical overhaul based on taxpayer-financed national health models or on universal social insurance.

The conservative contribution to the health care debate has been confined largely to criticizing liberal proposals.

This study attempts to fill that void. It offers a strategy to make adequate health care available at acceptable cost to every American within a framework where strong market incentives operate to give the widest possible degree of choice and the best possible value per dollar for both patients and taxpayers.

The key element in this reform strategy...is to address the core defects of the current system by turning today's quasi-market health care system into a true market system.

As this study makes clear, only a far-reaching set of market-based reforms, accompanied by a strong campaign to explain the reforms to the American people, will end that frustration and cure the ills of America's health care system.

Reform must create a health care system that satisfies the demands and priorities of the American people and does so in a way that encourages the health care market to adjust to the choices of consumers rather than frustrating the operation of markets. The current crisis in large part stems from the failure of lawmakers to view the system as a market.

A responsible reform must achieve the broad health care objectives of the American people in a manner that cures the structural problems of the current system. As such, it must reach three goals:

- Goal #1: A reformed U.S. health care system must give all Americans access to adequate health care services.

  America's current health care system contains unacceptable gaps in coverage. A reformed system must bridge these gaps.

- Goal #2: A reformed U.S. health care system must contain market-based incentives to moderate costs.

  Today's system is riddled with perverse incentives for rapid cost escalation. Congress has tried to staunch this by introducing ineffective and damaging price controls. Needed instead is a system that uses competition and price incentives to reduce inflationary pressures.

- Goal #3: While prices must be used to encourage the efficient use of health care resources, a reformed system must ensure that families do not suffer catastrophic financial losses because of ill health.

  The current system protects most Americans from most routine medical costs but leaves them unprotected against heavy costs. A reformed system must focus on catastrophic protection.

Enthoven A, Kronick R. A consumer-choice health plan for the 1990s: universal health insurance in a system designed to promote quality and economy. *N Engl J Med.* 1989;320:29-37, 94-101.

Reprinted with permission of *The New England Journal of Medicine.*

America's health care economy is a paradox of excess and deprivation. We spend more than 11 percent of the gross national product on health care, yet roughly 35 million Americans have no financial protection from medical expenses. To an increasing degree, the present financing system is inflationary, unfair, and wasteful. In its place we need a strategy that addresses the whole system, offers financial protection from health care expenses to all, and promotes the development of economical financing and delivery arrangements. Such a strategy must be designed to be broadly acceptable in our society.

To remedy the deprivation, we propose that everyone not covered by Medicare, Medicaid, or some other public program be enabled to buy affordable coverage, either through their employers or through a "public sponsor." To attack the excess, we propose a strategy of managed competition in which collective agents, called sponsors, such as the Health

Care Financing Administration and large employers, contract with competing health plans and manage a process of informed cost-conscious consumer choice that rewards providers who deliver high-quality care economically.

We describe the characteristics necessary for a plan for universal health insurance to find broad acceptance. Such a plan must represent incremental, not radical, change; must respect the preferences of voters, patients, and providers; must avoid major disruption in satisfactory existing arrangements; must avoid creating major windfall gains or losses; must avoid large-scale income redistribution; and must not be inflationary.

Our proposal would create a framework that would encourage the efficient organization of care. Successful organizations would probably be those that attracted the loyalty and commitment of physicians, integrated insurance and the provision of care, and aligned the interests of doctors and patients toward high-quality, cost-effective care. The proposal's chief potential disadvantage would be its effect on the employment opportunities of low-wage workers, but this effect could be minimized.

In addition, we discuss a proposal to mandate coverage by employers of full-time employees, legislation enacted recently in Massachusetts, high-risk pools, and the system followed in Canada, comparing each of these alternatives with our proposal.

Himmelstein DU, Woolhandler S, The Writing Committee of the Working Group on Program Design. A national health program for the United States: a physicians' proposal. *N Engl J Med.* 1989;320:102-108.

Our health care system is failing. Tens of millions of people are uninsured, costs are skyrocketing, and the bureaucracy is expanding. Patchwork reforms succeed only in exchanging old problems for new ones. It is time for basic change in American medicine. We propose a national health program that would (1) fully cover everyone under a single, comprehensive public insurance program; (2) pay hospitals and nursing homes a total (global) annual amount to cover all operating expenses; (3) fund capital costs through separate appropriations; (4) pay for physicians' services and ambulatory services in any of three ways: through fee-for-service payments with a simplified fee schedule and mandatory acceptance of the national health program payment as the total payment for a service or procedure (assignment), through global budgets for hospitals and clinics employing salaried physicians, or on a per capita basis (capitation); (5) be funded, at least initially, from the same sources as at present, but with all payments disbursed from a single pool; and (6) contain costs through savings on billing and bureaucracy, improved health planning, and the ability of the national health program, as the single payer for services, to establish overall spending limits. Through this proposal, we hope to provide a pragmatic framework for public debate for fundamental health-policy reform.

National Leadership Commission on Health Care. For the Health of a Nation: A Shared Responsibility. Ann Arbor, Michigan: Health Administration Press; 1989.

Reprinted with permission from the National Leadership Coalition for Health Care Reform.

Formed in 1986 by a group of concerned citizens to address the three major problems of cost, quality, and access to health care, the National Leadership Commission on Health Care proposes a major restructuring of the nation's health care system.

During its deliberations, the Commission agreed on a vision of a healthy society in the 21st century, one which promoted preventive care and healthy lifestyles through vigorous public education, and operates an innovative, efficient health care system that provides universal access to a basic level of appropriate, affordable care. The system would encourage personal responsibility for choosing good health and appropriate treatment, support a strong doctor-patient relationship, and promote a public-private partnership to control costs and constantly improve the quality of care. It would also find a solution to the malpractice crisis.

...the Commission proposes a new public/private partnership that will provide access for all to a health care system which will deliver cost-effective, appropriate care. Under our proposal, all Americans would be required to have health insurance coverage for a package of basic service.

Our model calls for a shared responsibility to finance care for the currently uninsured. It retains a significant role for the states and private insurance companies. It is structured to foster competition and innovation in the quality and efficient management of health care services. The plan calls for a strong education campaign to encourage patients to adopt healthy lifestyles and to inform patients and providers about guidelines for appropriate care to help them make better decisions about treatment.

The Commission's strategy, then, has the following critical, interrelated elements.

- *Provide universal access* through a Universal Access (UNAC) program to a basic level of health care, regardless of income.
- *Make individual Americans responsible* for having health insurance for at least a basic level of care.
- *Expand the existing insurance system* by encouraging all employers to provide health insurance for their employees.
- *Spread the cost* of universal access systematically among all individuals and employers who can afford to contribute and *make explicit now hidden costs*, with everyone paying a small premium for a basic level of care for those who cannot afford to pay.
- *Establish a nationally determined level of basic services* of health care available to all, allowing for state variations above that level.
- *Greatly increase research on the appropriateness, effectiveness, and quality of care* and publicize the results widely to help patients and providers assess treatment.
- *Control costs by reducing the amount of inappropriate care* as a result of the expanded research.
- *Encourage the marketplace* to work more efficiently by stimulating the development and use of solid information about appropriateness, quality, and cost, thus giving the private sector the tools to develop more efficient organizations of providers and other cost-effective delivery systems.
- *Develop a process for a strong public-private partnership* to improve quality and control costs by coordinating the expanded research on appropriateness and quality and disseminating the results through the health professional organizations.
- *Develop and continually update national guidelines* useful to practitioners in making clinical decisions, through the appropriate medical specialties.
- *Call on existing state agencies* to operate the program to finance care for the currently uninsured, negotiating fair compensation for providers who serve that population.
- *Promote nationwide the current, promising state reforms in malpractice.*

Shortell SM, McNerney WJ. Criteria and guidelines for reforming the U.S. health care system. *N Engl J Med.* 1990;322:463-466.

It would be tempting to suggest that the U.S. health care system is now in disarray were it not for the fact that it has never really been otherwise. There is increasing anger and frustration among employers, consumers, uninsured people, payers, and providers, all of whom are struggling with what are perceived to be competing demands to contain costs while trying to improve productivity, increase quality, and expand access to services. Clearly, our health care system needs more comprehensive strategies to address the multiple needs of different groups.

We do not lack for new ideas or alternative models....What we appear to lack, however, is the ability to put the concepts, ideas, and models together into a package that appeals to a suitably broad cross section of the American public. We are up against ourselves and our deeply held respect for autonomy and pluralism, which take on added importance in view of the great diversity of our culture.

The lack of focus in the debates on health policy and the proposals for reform is untenable. In the near future a variety of proposals for reform are likely to come from both public and private sources, and there is a legitimate basis for disagreement on the wisdom and probable efficacy of any one course of action. But the lessons of the past suggest a few of the necessary next steps. The medically disenfranchised must be included in basic health care. The criteria for both fiscal and clinical accountability must be met. Care must be linked to the defined needs of the population and made reasonably affordable through a number of sources of revenue. And there must be room for creativity and innovation in regard to specific delivery approaches. The criteria and guidelines proposed here meet these needs. Their aim is to produce a better-informed consumer and a more accountable provider, working with new ground rules within preestablished revenue limits based on defined needs.

U.S. Bipartisan Commission on Comprehensive Health Care. The Pepper Commission. A Call for Action. Washington, D.C.: U.S. Government Printing Office; 1990.

The Commission concludes that, in the absence of systemwide reform, the proportion of Americans without adequate health care coverage will grow. The burden of caring for those who cannot pay will overwhelm the system, putting us all at risk of inadequate access to care. As costs continue to rise, more and more dollars will go to services of uncertain value, while millions of people will go without basic and necessary care.

To prevent such a disaster, the Commission unanimously adopted the following goal:

The Commission is commited to the development of recommendations for public policies that will assure all Americans access to affordable health care coverage that allows them to obtain necessary care and assures them adequate financial protection; that will promote quality care and address the problem of health care costs; and that will provide the financing required to assure access.

...The Commission's blueprint for building a universal job-based/public system of health care coverage has five parts.

1. The Commission believes that employers and the government together should provide a minimum level of health care coverage for workers and nonworkers who, in turn, should be expected to accept that coverage....

2. The Commission believes that all parties — employers, individuals, and government — should share in financing health care coverage. Requirements for financial participation should not impose excessive burdens on individuals or employers. It is the federal government's responsibility to establish a ceiling on obligations related to ability to pay, and to provide the additional necessary financing. Therefore, *the Commission recommends that the small employers encouraged to provide coverage receive tax credits/subsidies to reduce the costs of private insurance; that employers required to provide coverage be able to obtain it from a federal program for a contribution set at a fixed share of their payroll expenses; and that low-income workers and nonworkers receive subsidies to keep their contributions within reasonable bounds.*

3. The Commission believes that private insurers and government should each play a role in administering health care coverage. But there is a critical need for reforms to strengthen both private and public performance, making coverage not only available but also adequate to ensure access to care. In

order to preserve and expand private insurance as the primary source of job-based coverage, *the Commisssion recommends requirements that would bring an end to the underwriting, rating, and marketing practices that are unraveling private insurance protection for small employers.* At the same time, *the Commission recommends that responsibility for providing public coverage be shifted from states to the federal government, be severed from the welfare system, be uniform across the country, and pay providers at rates determined by Medicare rules.*

4. The Commission believes that universal health care coverage that ensures people access to necessary care must meet an adequate minimum standard. That standard should establish basic protection for the currently uninsured and underinsured and preserve protection for the currently insured into the future. For public and private coverage, *the Commission recommends a federally specified minimum benefit package that includes preventive and primary care as well as other physician and hospital care.* Individuals would be responsible for a share of premiums and service costs—on all but preventive services—up to a maximum and subject to their ability to pay.

5. The Commission believes that action cannot come too soon for the millions without coverage and millions more who see their coverage threatened. However, an effective system cannot be put into place overnight. It will take time to develop and implement.

To balance these concerns, the Commission recommends that the system be put in place a step at a time.

COMMENTARY

Ronald P. Kaufman

T his section contains six key proposals relating to reform of the American health care system. Some of these proposals emanate from organizations or groups, and others from specific individuals. One must be cognizant that these six do not represent the universe of available proposals, nor is this section intended to be fully exhaustive. Predictably, over the next few years additional approaches will be developed and presented in a variety of forums, since health care is a critical issue for society and is becoming a more and more important issue in the political arena. For example, the Pepper Commission proposal is an important political statement, and parts of that report may be translated in the form of legislative initiatives in the near term.

These six proposals, nonetheless, do represent a very adequate sample of the full spectrum of the options available to address the issue of system reform. For example, the proposals range from a very conservative proposal from the Heritage Foundation that endorses a true market-based approach, suggesting that this is the more traditional American way of addressing such major societal issues, to a more radical restructuring outlined by Himmelstein and Woolhandler of the Physicians for a National Health Program. Between these two extremes, however, most of the proposals build on incremental change and suggest using the employer-based mandate of health insurance as the cornerstone for remedying the access problem. There are various approaches to the employer-based mandate, but most suggest a specific benefit package, bringing the program down to the state or regional level for administration, and some reliance on competitive forces between managed care plans as a key element for cost containment.

Irrespective of the solutions proposed, there is generally broad acceptance of the shortcomings of the current system. These shortcomings are primarily in three areas: continued uncontrolled inflationary costs; simultaneously increasing disenfranchisement, that is, a lack of access; and finally, a concern about quality and the lack of data relative to outcomes. The key variance in approach to reform, therefore, is whether one should conservatively and incrementally build on the current system, recognizing its intrinsic flaws, versus wholesale restructuring of the health care system and the concomitant risk of adopting untested approaches.

This reviewer will neither review and analyze each proposal nor offer a synopsis or a critique of the strengths or weaknesses of the individual plans. These types of analyses have been well done elsewhere by others. Moreover, the articles do, indeed, speak for themselves.

Rather, it is appropriate to focus serious commentary on whether the access issue can be adequately addressed through a financing system of private health insurance, primarily employment-based. Health insurance is not truly insurance, but rather is currently a tax-free benefit which, when available, "induces" demand. Before investing the majority of reform on an employer mandate, one must recognize the current problems that prevent health insurance, through employment, from achieving universal coverage. First of all, offering insurance as a benefit of employment is a market phenomenon. If employers need to offer such a benefit, they will; if they believe they can hire manpower without such a benefit, they tend not to offer it. It is partly for these reasons that small firms and low-wage earners frequently do not have insurance and will decline it if offered. In addition, employers can avoid the mandate by using more part-time workers or, worse yet, by reducing future wages of employees to cover the cost of the new health package rather than adding that cost to the price of their product, which parenthetically, in the international marketplace, might not be viable.

Secondly, private health insurance has not been able to achieve truly comprehensive coverage since preventive services and health promotional services that are frequently offered by non-physicians have not been actuarially researched, causing justifiable fear and concern within the insurance industry about moving in such a direction.

Third, insurance, being a third party, currently has and, in the view of many, will continue to have, significant difficulties in controlling the cost spiral. Current efforts at managed care and quality assurance have, to date, not truly demonstrated an ability to control cost escalation, despite the extraordinarily high administrative costs associated with those efforts, especially as compared to the Medicare program or the Canadian system.

Finally, the employer mandate might well result in a significant escalation of unemployment, currently estimated to be between five and eight million people. In conclusion, this reviewer believes that there is significant risk in making employer mandated health insurance the cornerstone of reform since there is evidence that such an approach might well be significantly flawed. Rather if cost, access, and quality are the appropriate concerns relative to the health care system, more fundamental restructuring should be sought.

Academic health centers will be impacted by these changes whether incremental or more radical in nature and, therefore, should be active participants in the process of policy formulation and implementation.

COMMENTARY

Richard L. O'Brien

The proposals for health care reform elucidate a broad consensus about the problems facing our society in providing adequate health care for all Americans at affordable cost. These proposals are in general agreement about the need to provide universal access to adequate health care, to ensure that health care is effective and of high quality, and to control costs so that value is received for resources expended.

Furthermore, there is general agreement on several elements intended to achieve these aims. Each proposal, either explicitly or implicitly, calls for a nationally determined set of minimum health care benefits, universal coverage, tax-supported subsidies for the poor, and managed care in one or another of its several forms. Some of these plans mandate employer provided insurance supplemented by subsidies for small businesses and the unemployed poor. Some attempt to sever health care insurance from employment.

One might think that with such consensus about the need to ensure access to adequate affordable care for all Americans, it should be relatively easy to design a system to achieve this end and to implement the means. However, the Utopian view fails to recognize the diversity of political, social, and economic philosophies underlying the proposals before us. Different philosophies result in proposals ranging from minimal government involvement and control, to government funded and administered national health insurance.

Because of different philosophies, and many competing interests, any plan proposed to reform the health care system will encounter significant opposition, based on self-interest and/or sincere belief in what will or will not work.

Perhaps the simplest and boldest proposal presented here is that described by Himmelstein and Woolhandler. This proposes a complete change of our existing health care system, introducing national health insurance covering all residents of the United States and encompassing essentially all providers. It is thoughtfully presented and acknowledges that there are problems in the existing system that their plan does not adequately address. Major opposition to this reform results from the fact that it would lead to the demise of a large fraction of existing private health insurance companies. Any consideration of this sort will engender tremendous political opposition by this interest group. Another problem is the proposal to link a global health care budget to gross national product. This arbitrary means of determining health care budgets is not rational. The gross national product comprises so many factors unrelated to health care and health care costs that may vary greatly without reference to other components of gross national product. It is as reasonable to link the health care budget to the price of oil or to fix the value of currency to some standard of health care services.

Perhaps the next most radical of the proposals presented here is that of the Heritage Foundation. It is based on a near religious faith that market place phenomena will result in good service, quality and cost control. It utilizes several strategies popular with political and economic conservatives, including reliance on individual responsibility (for the provision of health care insurance), vouchers for the poor to purchase services from the private sector, and need-based government subsidies. This group espouses mandating the purchase of health insurance by every household in the United States. The problems associated with this are almost too obvious: enforcement would be a nightmare and, for practical purposes, the plan is unlikely to deal with the needs of a large fraction of the existing, uninsured population.

Closer to a middle ground and the proposal that attempts to achieve maximum political feasibility and broad acceptance is the Consumer Choice Health Plan for the 1990s by Enthoven and Kronick. This plan builds on the current system and proposes to systematize and to extend cost control strategies already in wide use. It preserves the role of government, private insurance and the existing multiple means of reimbursing providers. The authors argue that systematic application of collective negotiating units, including employers, state governments, and insurance companies will result in slow, incremental evolution to a more efficient, less costly system that provides full cost-effective coverage of all Americans. They acknowledge that critics will argue that existing contracted and managed care programs are not controlling costs well; but the authors argue that these cost control strategies are not broadly or systematically applied.

The other proposals included in this volume are closely related in one way or another to these three, which represent the ends and the middle of the spectrum of political, social, and economic philosophies. That presented by the American College of Physicians, "Access to Health Care," probably provides the most thoughtful and systematic analysis of the problems facing American health care and the clearest definition of criteria to judge system reforms. However, the proposal stops short of meeting the existing problems it so aptly defines. Instead, it rather timidly suggests mandated employer provided health insurance, expansion of Medicaid, and continued study. It acknowledges that employer mandates and Medicaid expansions carry serious risks and may not succeed. It suggests that some form of "nationwide financing mechanism" may be necessary.

None of the proposals addresses certain problems, though some acknowledge them. All note the barrier to access represented by being uninsured or underinsured. However, these are no proposals here to deal with poor access related to specialty maldistribution or the provision of care to underserved populations. Several allude to increased costs related to the existing system for dealing with malpractice claims, but none proposes specific malpractice reform.

Only one of these plans acknowledges that health care reform should consider education of health care professionals. This should be of great concern to academic health centers. These institutions were able easily to extract adequate support for educational programs from the system until 1983. With the introduction of Medicare prospective payment and the wide expansion of contracted and managed care, it has become increasingly difficult to support the costs of education. When hospitals were reimbursed for costs and/or charges, academic health centers were able to spread education costs to all payers. Now, Medicare is making explicit efforts to decrease reimbursement for educational costs. Insurance companies explicitly or implicitly deny responsibility for educational costs. Thus, the costs of education are impossible to spread broadly and more difficult to support. System reform must take the education of health professionals into consideration or we run the risk of producing inadequate numbers of well-trained health professionals.

Most who observe our health care system believe that the definition of problems and alternate solutions have been well elucidated. Not much will be added by more analysis and new reform proposals. So, where do we go from here?

All proposed plans of which I am aware call for a central role for the federal government. All call for the government to define a set of minimum health care benefits and to mandate that all Americans be covered by adequate health care insurance. Several pieces of legislation introduced in the United States Congress provide clear evidence that some in Congress have accepted the responsibility.

The exact shape of legislated reform is likely to emerge from public and political debate and the negotiations that are certain to ensue. Given the acuity of the problems facing the health care system (in particular, cost) and the near universal agreement about the need for reform, it is likely that this political process will produce a new or modified system. It will not be perfect nor will it address all problems with equal efficacy. It is also likely to be a continuing process; our society tends to support evolutionary or incremental change with frequent adjustments to correct errors.

Thus, we may expect to see vigorous political discourse, acrimonious at times. There will be reform, some of which will be good, some of which will produce more harm than good. There is also likely to be short-term disruption and possibly pain in parts of the system. It is almost certain to be a messy process. But, that is the American way.

CHAPTER VI

International Comparisons

ABSTRACTS AND EXCERPTS

Day P, Klein R. The politics of modernization:
Britain's national health service in the 1980s.
Milbank Q. 1989;67:1-34.

For 40 years following its creation in 1948, Britain's National Health Service (NHS) institutionalized a particular vision of health care delivery. It was a remarkably stable model based on the values of rational, bureaucratic paternalism. The benefits of medical science were to be applied and distributed by the professional experts; funding and structure were, in turn, designed to give the greatest possible scope and autonomy to these experts, so allowing the twin objectives of universal coverage and financial control to be achieved....The publication in January 1989 of the Government's White Paper on the NHS, *Working for Patients...*, hereinafter referred to as the Review, marked the beginning of a new era. It was presented by the Government as the embodiment of a new millenarian vision, a design for health care delivery in the twenty-first century which would marry old-style British ideals of social justice with new-style American ideas about competition, and combine capped budgets with consumer choice.

Seen from the inside, and in particular from the perspective of the medical profession, the NHS is in process of change unprecedented in its history. What we have, then, is the picture of an institution where, behind the stately facade, the workmen are beginning to gut the old building and to modernize it.

...the Review offers a field day for speculation. Specifically, the impact of the two most radical proposals, those for self-governing hospitals and GP budget holders, is contingent on the willingness of hospital staff and general practitioners to enter the new world of the medical market and to engage in that most unprofessional of all activities, competition. In turn, their willingness will depend on the availability of the information technology necessary for proper budgetary control (at present lacking in NHS), and the likely balance of risks and incentives. No one knows, though many speculate, about the likely impact of allowing hospitals to fix their own salary levels; might not the result be to push up NHS staffing costs? No one knows, though many speculate, whether the effect of the proposals will be to encourage the growth of the private sector or whether it will persuade NHS hospitals to engage in cutthroat competition. Above all, no one knows whether independent hospitals and budget-holding GPs will eventually become the norm or whether these will remain experimental eccentrics. No one knows, too, the long-term effects of moving from a NHS based on trust to one based on contract, from a closed system of self-regulation by the professional providers to a more open system of audit with a strong managerial influence. Only one prediction seems reasonably safe. This is that, to the extent that Britain follows the United States, so the new era will benefit the middlemen of health care: researchers, accountants, financial and management consultants, and others who profess expertise about efficiency even if they do not necessarily add to it.

Evans RG, Lomas J, Barer ML, et al. Controlling health expenditures—the Canadian reality. *N Engl J Med.* 1989;320:571-577.

Reprinted with permission of *The New England Journal of Medicine.*

Canada and the United States have conducted a large-scale social experiment on the effects of alternative ways of funding expenditures for health care. Two very similar societies, with (until recently) very similar systems of providing health care, have adopted radically different systems of reimbursement. The results of this experiment are of increasing interest to Americans, because the Canadian approach has avoided or solved several of the more intractable problems facing the United States. In particular, overall health expenditures have been constrained to a stable share of national income, and universality of coverage (without user charges) eliminates the problems of uncompensated care, individual burdens of catastrophic illness, and uninsured populations.

The combination of cost control with universal, comprehensive coverage has surprised some American observers, who have questioned its reality, its sustainability, or both. We present a comparison of the Canadian and American data on expenditures, identifying the sectors in which the experience of the two nations diverges most, and describing the processes of control. In any system, cost control involves conflict between providers and payers. Political processes focus this conflict, whereas market processes diffuse it. But the stylized political combat in Canada may result in less intrusion on the professional autonomy of the individual physician than is occurring in the United States.

Fuchs VR, Hahn JS. How does Canada do it? A comparison of expenditures for physician services in the United States and Canada. *N Engl J Med.* 1990;323:884-890.

Reprinted with permission of *The New England Journal of Medicine.*

As a percentage of the gross national product, expenditures for health care in the United States are considerably larger than in Canada, even though one in seven Americans is uninsured whereas all Canadians have comprehensive health insurance. Among the sectors of health care, the difference in spending is especially large for physicians' services. In 1985, per capita expenditure was $347 in the United States and only $202 (in U.S. dollars) in Canada, a ratio of 1.72. We undertook a quantitative analysis of this ratio.

We found that the higher expenditures per capita in the United States are explained entirely by higher fees; the quantity of physicians' services per capita is actually lower in the United States than in Canada. U.S. fees for procedures are more than three times as high as Canadian fees; the difference in fees for evaluation and management services is about 80 percent. Despite the large difference in fees, physicians' net incomes in the United States are only about one-third higher than in Canada. A parallel analysis of Iowa and Manitoba yielded results similar to those for the United States and Canada, except that physicians' net incomes in Iowa are about 60 percent higher than in Manitoba. Updating the analysis to 1987 on the basis of changes in each country between 1985 and 1987 yielded results similar to those obtained for 1985.

We suggest that increased use of physicians' services in Canada may result from universal insurance coverage and from encouragement of use by the larger number of physicians who are paid lower fees per service. U.S. physicians' net income is not increased as much as the higher U.S. fees would predict, probably because of greater overhead expenses and the lower workloads of America's procedure-oriented physicians.

Iglehart JK. Canada's health care system faces its problems. N Engl J Med. 1990;322:562-568.

Reprinted with permission of *The New England Journal of Medicine*.

Canada's provincial health insurance plans have demonstrated an impressive capacity to operate successfully despite a basic policy conflict that says health care funding must be public and universal, physicians must retain their professional autonomy, consumers must have free choice of doctors and first-dollar coverage, and provincial governments must control their budgets. But now provinces are finding it increasingly difficult to maintain this equation, because a variety of factors are perturbing its balance. In the face of a large budget deficit, the national government continues to reduce its financial commitment to the plans, patients and practitioners are demanding better access to the latest forms of medical technology, the supply of physicians continues to increase at a rate outstripping the growth of the population, and doctors are restive as provinces work more aggressively to stem the rise in health expenditures.

Canada's health care system is buffeted by conflicting forces—its strong commitment to universal access, of which Canadians are justifiably proud; the accelerating efforts of the provinces to control costs while they continue to expand the scope of covered benefits; and the increasing frustration of practicing physicians and hospital stewards who are caught in the middle. Until recently, these tensions have remained within manageable bounds throughout Canada, but whether that will continue, without a new accommodation, particularly if the national economy slows, is an open question.

Revising the current formulation of policy will require a more meaningful dialogue than exists at present among the federal and provincial governments, organized medicine, and other major stakeholders in the system. Without such dialogue, Canadians place at risk the future of their provincial health insurance plans, social enterprises that are admired throughout the Western world. The medical profession faces an additional challenge: to examine more rigorously the appropriateness and efficacy of the clinical care it renders.

Iglehart JK. The United States looks at Canadian health care. *N Engl J Med.* **1989;321:1767-1772.**

Reprinted with permission of *The New England Journal of Medicine.*

Health insurance programs reflect the cultural beliefs, political priorities, and medical imperatives of the countries in which they evolve. Across a continuum that features more or less reliance on government or private mechanisms, most Western countries have concluded that the financial consequences of illness should be borne by societies, not individuals. That is certainly the case in Canada, which provides all its 25.6 million citizens with access to medical care, but does not charge them directly for the services they receive. Specifically, Canada places responsibility squarely on its government to finance a comprehensive set of medical benefits and prohibits private sources of funding; but private fee-for-service physicians provide the bulk of the care and do so with a high degree of clinical autonomy.

Although there is little thought that Canada's scheme could be replicated here, its very presence in North America, where it can be readily observed and studied, increases pressure on the United States to remedy the widely perceived flaws in its own medical care system. This pressure comes not only from public officials, but also from a growing number of private payers (like Chrysler Corporation and Ford Motor Company), which seem prepared to delegate more responsibility to government as a way of controlling the cost of the comprehensive benefits they have negotiated with organized labor.

The United States, on the other hand, has shied away from many of the tough issues that confront our health care system, falling back on its belief in limited government, its reliance on private markets as the favored instrument of allocation except for the categorical programs serving elderly, disabled, and poor Americans and war veterans, and the seeming illusion that somehow we can have it all without explicitly addressing the imbalances in access, cost, and quality that currently characterize U.S. medicine. Regardless of whether future U.S. health care policy should be guided by more governmental or more private-sector activity, we must develop society-wide policies to allocate resources more equitably and systematically, as have all other Western countries. Muddling through, as we are now doing, is not a prescription for the ages, nor is it a policy that allows the United States to stand tall.

Linton AL. A Canadian physician's perspective. *N Engl J Med.* 1990;322:197-199.

Reprinted with permission of *The New England Journal of Medicine.*

Canada is perceived to have one of the best health care systems in the developed world, publicly funded and providing universal coverage. It has avoided the direct governmental controls of Britain's National Health Service and the increasingly close monitoring of medical decisions by third-party payers in the United States.

Before attempting to duplicate the Canadian system, however, Americans would be wise to look closely for flaws that may just be beginning to emerge.

Canada's health care system may have given us a few years of universal, affordable health care during a period when the U.S. experiment with competition failed to control costs or guarantee accessibility. It is sensible for Americans to look at the Canadian system, but they should not be blind to the risks inherent in government-controlled monopoly, nor should they ignore the evidence suggesting that we can no longer expect current structures to continue to control costs. It is ironic that as the United States looks at the Canadian system, the British government is moving rapidly toward competition and a modified U.S. system in an attempt to reduce further the costs of the already parsimonious National Health Service. At the same time, several Canadian provinces are completing the circle by attempting to introduce concepts from the National Health Service into the Canadian system.

Perhaps all structural tinkering is doomed to fail. The root causes of the problem are the increase in demand and the explosion of new forms of technology. These make the rationing of health care inevitable and the chief issue we should be addressing publicly.

Lister J. Reform of the British National Health Service: from white paper to bill in Parliament. *N Engl J Med.* 1990;322:410-412.

Reprinted with permission of *The New England Journal of Medicine.*

As anticipated, the proposals for reforming the British National Health Service (NHS) that were announced in January 1989 in a government white paper entitled "Working for Patients" have been widely debated....it was proposed that general practitioners (family physicians) in group practices with more than 11,000 registered patients should be encouraged to become "budget holders," able to contract with hospitals for the care of their patients. Hospitals would be allowed to apply to become NHS trusts with self-governing status. Instead of relying on the Health Authorities for their funds, they would then generate income by contracting with family doctors and with other hospitals in both the NHS and the private sector to provide services to patients for established fees.

Apart from these proposals, the white paper emphasized the need for greater accountability among doctors in both general practice and hospitals and for the establishment of formalized systems of medical audit in order to account for wide variations in clinical practice and outcome in different hospitals and to assess the value of new forms of technology.

Within the profession, meanwhile, morale has undoubtedly suffered on account of the uncertainty over the future of the NHS and the prospect that the service may become destabilized. This is an aspect of the whole affair that the politicians may have been unwise to overlook, because although doctors may never have been popular with the politicians, no health service can function effectively without their cooperation.

Schieber GJ, Poullier JP. Health expenditures in major industrialized countries, 1960-87. *Health Care Financing Review.* 1990;11:159-167.

...even after adjusting for inflation within countries, U.S. real per capita health spending was the highest in the world and the gap between the United States and Canada, the second highest country, has widened. In other words, the volume and intensity of health services provided to Americans has been by far the highest in the world and has increased as fast or faster than in other high-expenditure countries.

Although differences in performance may be related to differences in underlying morbidity, amenities, economic efficiency, and/or quality, the current state of the art in international comparisons and health services research cannot measure these factors or attribute differences in these factors to specific features of health systems. Nevertheless, these comparisons raise difficult questions for U.S. policymakers. Has reliance on competition, freedom of choice, and entrepreneurship provided Americans with the best health care system in the world? Would the impersonality, queuing, and lack of choice inherent in some other countries' health systems be an acceptable trade-off to the American public for more economic efficiency and greater equity?

Walker MA. From Canada: a different viewpoint. *Health Management Q*. 1989;11:11-14.

Reprinted with permission from *Health Management Quarterly*.

The most attractive aspect of the Canadian health-care system and the one that explains why it is consistently the most popular program among Canadians is the fact that it provides access with no apparent cost.

Unlike other markets, where increased demand is welcomed because it brings an increase in revenues, increased demand in Canada's medical markets brings only increased demand for part of the provincial government's budget. Whether to respond with an increase in resources then becomes a purely political decision as health care competes with asphalt laying and university funding in the calculus of governments.

The reason costs have escalated to a much greater degree in the United States is because there has not been an across-the-board cap placed on health-care spending. Increased demand in the United States has meant an increase in total health-care spending, not shortages, waiting lists and decline in the quality of care. It is far from clear that this should be decried, especially given the increasing evidence from Canada about the alternatives.

Robert J. Joynt

One of the highest priorities of many countries is to find the best health care system for its people. The desirable elements of such a system are universal access and high quality care at a low cost. It has not been demonstrated that these can be achieved by any extant system if you also include freedom of choice of provider and services, ease and convenience of access, no or minimal waiting, no rationing of services, and adequate reimbursement to the provider. If all the elements are interjected into the formula, low cost is no longer attainable in the different national systems now in operation. Therefore, most systems have modified these elements with varying success. Unfortunately, the United States has one of the least desirable modifications—that of limiting access because of no or inadequate health insurance. In addition, we have the highest health costs per capita of seven industrial countries analyzed by Schieber. In spite of measures to control expenditures, the gap between our spending and that of other nations is increasing. Schieber concludes, "perhaps it is time to take a closer look at some of the features of these systems that have created universal access at low cost without any demonstrable lower level of quality."

The "closer look" suggested by Schieber has been and will continue to be one of the primary responsibilities of academic health centers. These centers have been major contributors to the success and shortcomings of our health care system. High levels of patient care and great technological and scientific advances have made these centers models to the world. The failure with limited access and inadequate delivery of care while due to many social, political, and economic factors must also be part of academic health centers' responsibilities. Because of these shortcomings we must examine other systems, offer alternatives, devise demonstrations, and influence policymakers.

The papers included in this section look closely at two systems. The first which we have watched and analyzed for over 40 years is the National Health Service (NHS) in Britain. It is now undergoing extensive review with possible reforms so it is an appropriate time to look at its successes and problems. The second system is that of Canada, increasingly touted by Americans as the most desirable plan to pursue. Another system that is not known as well in this country is that of Germany. It has some features different from the other two and will be briefly mentioned.

The NHS was initiated after World War II. Despite major criticisms, it has survived since 1948 without major changes. But now there are major reforms put forth by the Government's White Paper, *Working for Patients*, that was published in 1989. The events that preceded these proposals took place largely during the Thatcher years and reflect the mood of privatization, freer choice, and more competition.

The publication of these proposals for reform has unleashed severe criticisms from some sectors of the medical profession. First, there are major concerns that very little input to the reforms was solicited from physicians. Second, it is proposed that hospitals and general practitioners should be free to make contractual arrangements and many physicians believe services will be directed or curtailed at the expense of good patient care. The 190 health districts in the United Kingdom would essentially become free-market HMOs. A major problem is there has been very little close scrutiny linking resources to outcome so that experience is grossly inadequate in this area. Other analysts raise the warning that as we contemplate more government control we should learn from Britain's recent experiences that led up to the proposed reforms and the problems those reforms may have created.

The Canadian health system is increasingly cited by the media and the American public as the way to proceed. As with many popular movements, insufficient knowledge does not stifle enthusiasm. The public view of various health care systems was described in a survey of citizens from 10 industrialized countries. The survey showed Canadian citizens best satisfied and Americans least satisfied. It also showed an increasing number of Americans preferring the Canadian system to their own.

The Canadian system differs from Britain's NHS in that the Canadian government through the provinces is the payer and not the provider. The NHS became both payer and provider. Evans and his colleagues compare the American and Canadian systems and conclude that the major difference is the degree of centralization of the cost-control process. The battle between the provider and payer is much more large scale in Canada as there is only the single payer, thus public awareness and consumer pressures are more effective. Per capita spending for physicians' services is higher in the United States than in Canada at a ratio of 1.72. This is accounted for by higher fees even though delivery of services is less. Incomes of American physicians are higher, but the difference is less than the ratio as overhead is higher. This is partly due to the complexity of billing with multiple payers.

Iglehart notes that the Canadian system with universal access and lower costs is attracting increasing attention by our lawmakers, many of whom are proposing comprehensive health care legislation such as that proposed by the Pepper Commission. He also reviews the features of the Canadian system that raise concerns by American providers. In a subsequent article, Iglehart details some of the difficulties with the Canadian system and points out that a major one is the reduced ability to change with changing circumstances as with the advent of new and better technology.

Canadian perspectives on their own system emphasize increasing concern over several issues. The government as the single payer has a great advantage when it bargains with the providers—physicians and hospitals. Recently, for example, the Ontario government has reduced the number of residents by fiat and will only pay for those working with physicians who do not charge fee-for-service outside of the capped-payment system. Walker, a Canadian economist, contends that the strict cost control has seriously affected the appropriate accessibility to services, which may lead to a reduction in quality.

The German health care system is currently under study by many experts. It depends on a regulated system of self-governing and self-financed sickness funds. These funds use premiums to redistribute income so that the sick and low-income groups are covered. Along with this are strictly regulated physician and hospital fees. The system avoids some of the less desirable parts of the Canadian system while providing a non-government system of pay.

The pursuit of the *healthy grail* is unending but necessary. The academic health centers have the ability and the responsibility to lead this quest.

COMMENTARY

M. David Low

T here is no longer any serious debate that the United States health care system is in desperate need of change. When the American Medical Association, the AFL-CIO, Chrysler Corporation, Consumer Reports, Paine Webber, Uwe Reinhardt, the Texas Medical Association, countless commissions, committees, citizens action groups, and the President of the United States all say so, then we have consensus. We must expand access, contain costs, preserve or enhance quality, and stop doing things that are inappropriate or of no benefit. Unfortunately, there is no consensus about how to achieve any of these goals individually, or even which to try first (let alone how to have them all together).

Access is the most urgent issue for most for us. Costs are a real problem to some, but apparently not to all. Everyone is for quality, either maintained or improved, but nobody knows for sure how to measure it (not even those who persist in equating it to dollars spent on provider services or to the availability of technology). There is great interest in appropriateness and effectiveness, but while this country will spend considerable money over the next decades trying to demonstrate whether selected medical and surgical procedures are either appropriate or effective, the payback can only be long-term.

Many have argued that we should examine the experience of other countries, pointing out that virtually every other nation in the developed world (excepting South Africa) has managed to provide universal or near-universal access to good quality health care while incurring costs which are much lower than ours. Canada has received the greatest attention, and much of the material in this section deals with its system. Because so much has been written both in praise and in criticism of the Canadian system, one might conclude that the subject has been exhausted. I believe, however, that there is at least one further way to look at Canadian health care that may bring into sharper focus changes that should be made in the U.S. system. Rather than continuing to look safely at the mechanics of the Canadian system, we ought to look at the principles underlying its creation and at what has been gained, lost or preserved in the process.

When the Canadian government took the momentous decision to

make every resident of the country equal before the health care system (equivalent to the principle of equality before the law), it did so after considerable debate ranging over nearly a quarter of a century, which concluded in 1968 when the Hall Commission answered the question "What is the *right* thing to do?" (not, "What is doable, or politically achievable?"). Such a question will not be easy to answer in the pluralistic society that is America, but I believe that we must try.

In trying to answer the question, it might be helpful to look at medical care on this continent in a ethical/historical context. In the "golden years" of the 1960s, the practice of medicine in the United States and Canada was essentially identical, as were the values held by the two health care systems (principally physicians): professional autonomy (society granted them an astonishing degree of it); individual autonomy (the patient could choose physicians, hospitals, and mode of care); advocacy (the physician's only responsibility was to the patient and the patient's welfare); and charity (physicians generally cared for all who came, regardless of ability to pay). Quality was largely defined by what the doctor did, and by the opinions of his colleagues.

Access to care was also an ideal in both countries, and in 1965— nearly simultaneously—the United States established the Medicare and Medicaid programs (all that could be salvaged from a failed attempt to introduce national health insurance), and Canada appointed the Hall Commission, which would recommend the creation of the Canadian health insurance plan in 1968.

Health care delivery remained very similar in the two countries until the end of the decade of the 1960s, and the aggregate cost of care, expressed as a percentage of the gross national product (GNP), was little different in Canada and the United States. By 1971, however, the year that the universal access plan was fully implemented in Canada, things began to change; over the next 15 years the two systems became dramatically different.

America experienced profound erosion on the ideals of health care through the appearance of for-profit health care, expansion of physician-owned services, integration of provider organizations, the establishment of managed care in the form of HMOs and PPOs, preadmission certification, utilization review, DRGs, changes in financing with a shift away from retrospective fee-for-service to prospective payment and salary. It is not clear yet whether the consequences have been fully appreciated. Physician autonomy, physician advocacy, patient autonomy, doctor and patient choice and access have all suffered. Rather than moving closer to the ideals that even in the 1960s were never fully realized, American health care has moved further away. At the same time, the cost of care has soared to well over $2,000 per capita (nearly 12 percent of the GNP), and more than 30 million Americans are shut out of the system.

In Canada, by contrast, citizens received virtually universal access to first-dollar, no limit, comprehensive hospital and medical services. The provincially run insurance plans preserved freedom of choice, all of the most important aspects of physician autonomy, and virtually hassle-free, fee-for-service payment. And medical practice remained a popular career option for young Canadians. The price was a limitation on diffusion of high-technology equipment and procedures, a moderate income disparity between Canadian surgeons (and some other specialists) and their American counterparts, a permanent public debate over the funding of health care (an essential feature of any system that might constrain costs, but desirable because the public always knows who is responsible for things being as they are), and a change of focus for the health insurance companies that had been in business prior to 1971. Aggregate health care costs rose to slightly less than $1,500 per capita (about 8.7 percent of the GNP). The difference between this figure and what we are paying in the United States is not trivial—it is in fact about equivalent to the annual budgetary deficit (prompting one to ask, what are we really getting for that cost?).

Taken altogether, it is arguable that the changes in the health system in Canada over the past two decades have moved that country closer to the ideals that at one time were so important to all of us. If we in America could answer that same very important question, "What is the right thing to do?" we too could once again move our system closer to the ideals that seemed so clear in 1960s.

CHAPTER VII

Quality, Outcomes, and Effectiveness of Care

ABSTRACTS AND EXCERPTS

Brook RH. Practice guidelines and practicing medicine: are they compatible? *JAMA* 1989;262:3027-3030.

Various factors, including increased financial pressures on the health system, the rapidity of the introduction of technology, and data showing high levels of inappropriate care, will coalesce into a movement that will yield practice guidelines. If the guidelines are developed with the aid of the best methods and if they are applied constructively, then the twin goals of increased health of the American public and physician satisfaction can be achieved.

To avoid repeating our mistakes, we must create an institution that is capable of developing and maintaining practice guidelines for both common diagnoses and common procedures. Such an institution does not currently exist. The mission of the institution would not only be the development of such guidelines, but also testing them and reporting, on a periodic cycle, the results of their application. All guidelines would be outcome based and outcome justified.

What will happen if such information were made available on a routine basis? (1) Policy could be altered so that resources are better directed to need.... (2) The information, when displayed over time, might be used by local institutions, or groups of physicians, as a stimulus and means to self-improvement. (3) The information might be provided to the public on an institutional or provider basis, perhaps in the form of a consumer report.... (4) New textbooks of medicine organized around guidelines might be developed and the whole educational process could be altered, including a greatly expanded role for the information sciences in medical school.... (5) Professional societies might develop performance-based review systems that would form the core of both their educational and recertification processes.... (6) Licensing bodies could base relicensing on compliance with guidelines and appropriateness standards. (7) Third-party payers could base their concept of a preferred provider and preferred organization on the above guidelines.... (8) Third-party payers could use the information prospectively and deny or question reimbursement for care, after physician review and appeal, that does not fulfill the guidelines. (9) Patients and physicians could use the information cooperatively and could better share decision making.... (10) The legal system could base malpractice decisions on the guidelines, and by knowing what was expected, malpractice claims and rates could decline.

If any or all of the above come true, then medicine will have changed.

Brook RH, Kambert CJ, Lohr KN, et al. Quality of ambulatory care: epidemiology and comparison by insurance status and income. *Medical Care.* 1990;23:392-433.

Reprinted with permission of J. B. Lippincott Co.

In this report the data from medical history questionnaires, screening examinations, insurance claims, and a face-to-face physician interview were used to examine the quality of ambulatory care received for 17 chronic conditions by a general population of 5986 adults ($\leq$65) and children ($\leq$14) enrolled in the RAND Health Insurance Experiment. Subjects in six U.S. sites were randomly assigned to insurance plans that were free or that required cost sharing, or in one site to an HMO. Quality-of-care criteria—both process (what was done to patients) and outcome (what happened to them)—were developed. Overall, 81% of outcome criteria and 62% of process criteria were met. Physicians interviewed patients with selected conditions at the Experiment's end to evaluate care. They suggested that approximately 70%

of patients should have their current therapy changed, but only 30% of patients would obtain more than minor improvement from such a change. Clinically meaningful plan differences in quality of care were observed only for the process criteria dealing with the need for a visit (free plan compliance 59%; cost sharing compliance 52%). Quality of care for the poor was slightly worse than for the nonpoor and persons randomized to an HMO had slightly better overall quality of care than those in the fee-for-service system. Substantial improvements in the quality of the process of care could be made, but impact on outcome may be small. Results of the analysis suggest the need for development of clinical models to test the relationship between specific process criteria and improvements in outcome.

Califf RM, Harrell FE, Lee KL, et al. The evolution of medical and surgical therapy for coronary artery disease: a 15-year perspective. *JAMA*. 1989;261:2077-2086.

To elucidate the factors associated with improved survival following coronary artery bypass surgery, we studied 5809 patients receiving medical or surgical therapy for coronary artery disease. Three factors were associated with a significant surgical survival benefit: more severe coronary disease, a worse prognosis with medical therapy, and a more recent operative date. Patients with more extensive coronary obstruction had the greatest improvement in survival. Patients with a poor prognosis because of factors such as older age, severe angina, or left ventricular dysfunction had a reduction in risk that was proportionate to their overall risk on medical therapy. Survival with surgery progressively improved over the study period and by 1984 surgery was significantly better than medical therapy for most patient subgroups. Thus, contemporary coronary revascularization is associated with improved longevity in many patients with ischemic heart disease, especially in those with adverse prognostic indicators.

Eddy DM. The challenge. *JAMA*. 1990;263:287-290.

Medical practice is in the middle of a profound transition. Most physicians can remember the day when, armed with a degree, a mission, and confidence, they could set forth to heal the sick. Like Solomon, physicians could receive patients, hear their complaints, and determine the best course of action. While not every patient could be cured, everyone could be confident that whatever was done was the best possible. Most important, each physician was free, trusted, and left alone to determine what was in the best interest of each patient.

All of that is changing.

What is going on is that one of the basic assumptions underlying the practice of medicine is being challenged....The challenge says that while many decisions no doubt are correct, many are not, and elaborate mechanisms are needed to determine which are which. Physicians are slowly being stripped of their decision-making power.

Why is the assumption that physicians' decisions are correct being challenged? At first thought, the challenge might appear to be a pernicious scheme launched by payers, motivated to save money, even at the expense of quality. Actually, while the rapid and apparently uncontrollable rise in health care costs might have been the initial pressure point, the challenge can be justified solely by a concern for quality. The plain fact is that many decisions made by physicians appear to be arbitrary—highly variable, with no obvious explanation. The very disturbing implication is that this arbitrariness represents, for at least some patients, suboptimal or even harmful care.

What is the evidence that decisions are arbitrary? The most impressive clues come in the form of variations across and within physicians with respect to observations, perceptions, reasoning, conclusions, and practices.

The solution is not to remove the decision-making power from physicians, but to improve the capacity of physicians to make better decisions. To achieve this solution, we must give physicians the information they need; we must institutionalize the skills to use that information; and we must build processes that support, not dictate, decisions.

Eddy DM. Anatomy of a decision. *JAMA*. 1990; 263:441-443.

The quality of medical care is determined by two main factors: the quality of the decisions that determine what actions are taken and the quality with which those actions are executed—what to do and how to do it.

The importance of ensuring the quality of execution is well understood. In contrast, the medical profession has done much less to develop and evaluate its decision-making processes.

...what can we reasonably expect physicians to be able to do? Begin with the second step—the value judgments. If physicians are provided good information regarding how alternative practices affect the outcomes that are important to patients, physicians can discuss that information with their patients and either help them evaluate the options and make a decision for themselves, or, if patients choose to delegate the decision, make it for them.

On the other hand, it is not realistic to expect physicians to be able to estimate the outcomes of different decisions accurately. This task requires access to research results, analytic skills, and time; none of which are readily available to practicing physicians. The analysis of evidence and estimation of outcomes is a discipline in itself, requiring about as much training as is needed to train a physician.

The solution is to analyze as many decision as possible in advance, potentially taking whatever time, resources, and skills are needed to make the most accurate estimates of the outcomes of alternative practices, and then pass this information to practicing physicians. This is the role of practice policies.

Eddy DM. Practice policies—what are they? *JAMA*. 1990;263:877-880.

Practice policies are preformed recommendations issued for the purpose of influencing decisions about health interventions. The basic problem addressed by practice policies is that most health decisions are too complicated to be made on a one-by-one, day-to-day basis.

Practice policies can have immense leverage. One well-designed policy—such as washing hands between deliveries—can improve the quality of care of hundreds of thousands of patients. Conversely, a poorly designed policy—such as performing lobotomies for the treatment of schizophrenia—can spoil the quality of care for just as many. A shift in a single policy—such as screening women younger than 50 years with mammography—can shift a billion dollars a year. Practice policies have the power to shape behavior for decades. A statement by a single practitioner in 1916 that "once a caesarean, always a caesarean" still dominates that decision.

...the role of practice policies has been shifting away from serving as passive aids to decisions, available to practitioners for use as they see fit, to being used as active management tools. Practice policies now are being designed explicitly as instruments for quality assurance, precertification, utilization review, accreditation, coverage, and cost containment.

But the greatest concern pertains to control. It is not stretching things too far to say that whoever controls practice policies controls medicine. That control used to lie exclusively, if diffusely, within the medical profession. However, as policies are designed and used as management tools, control could shift outside the profession. This possibility is a major force behind the surge of interest in practice policies.

Eddy DM. Practice policies: where do they come from? *JAMA*. 1990;263:1265-1275.

The purpose of a practice policy is to anticipate and simplify decisions that would otherwise have to be made on a one-by-one basis by individual physicians and their patients. Thus, the tasks involved in the design of a policy correspond to the two steps used by individuals for their personal decisions: estimation of the effects of a practice on outcomes important to patients and comparison of the outcomes of the practice to determine whether its benefits outweigh its harms and whether its health outcomes are worth its costs. The specific tasks are (1) identify the important health outcomes, (2) analyze evidence for the effects of the practice on those outcomes, (3) estimate the magnitudes of the outcomes (benefits and harms), (4) compare the benefits and harms, (5) estimate the costs, (6) compare the health outcomes with the costs, and (7) compare alternative practices to determine which deserve priority. As with decisions made by individuals, all of these tasks are performed, explicitly or implicitly, every time a practice policy is designed.

Eddy DM. Practice policies—guidelines for methods. *JAMA.* 1990;263:1839-1841.

Dozens of programs have been created during the last few years to design policies for medical practices, and more are being created every month. They use very different methods and produce very different documents....Obvious questions arise: Is there a "correct" method for designing a practice policy? Are there any minimal requirements for a policy statement? In general, what standards should we require our policies to meet?

In general, the formality of a method will depend on four factors: the importance of the health problem (eg, number of patients, severity of the outcomes, cost) the potential for harm that could be caused if a policy is incorrect, the simplicity of the clinical question, and the nature of the available evidence.

Because the guidelines for methods leave it to policymakers to choose methods capable of delivering the information needed for intelligent decisions, it is essential that policymakers expose their methods to review. The vehicle for this is the policy statement.

Eddy DM. Guidelines for policy statements: the explicit approach. *JAMA.* 1990;263:2239-2243.

The first obligation of a policymaker is to design a policy that, if accepted and applied correctly, will improve patients' lives. The second obligation is to present the policy in a way that ensures it will be accepted and applied correctly. The first obligation is addressed through the choice of methods for designing a policy. The second obligation is addressed through the policy statement.

To summarize, with the exception of the policymakers' natural desire to simplify their work load, the interests of all parties point in the same direction: a policy statement should not only describe the recommended action, but should describe the rationale for the recommendation and the consequences of following it.

Eddy DM. Comparing benefits and harms: the balance sheet. *JAMA*. 1990;263:2493-2505.

The central elements of a decision about a medical activity, and therefore the central elements of a policy statement, are the consequences of the interventions that are being considered—their benefits, harms, and costs. The estimates of health and economic outcomes condense the information from clinical research and clinical experience into a form suitable for decisions and provide the basis for judgments about the desirability of the intervention.

A simple but powerful way to present information on the outcomes of an intervention is the balance sheet.

To a great extent, we do not have good information to fill out balance sheets today, because we did not ask the right questions yesterday. To have the information we will need for decisions tomorrow, we must ask those questions today. An important goal for the next 5 years is to develop balance sheets for the 1000 most important clinical decisions.

Eddy DM. Designing a practice policy: standards, guidelines, and options. *JAMA*. 1990;263:3077-3084.

Designing a practice policy is similar to making a decision for an individual patient. In both cases, one must identify the available options, estimate the consequences of the different options, and determine the desirability of those outcomes to patients. Practice policies can be thought of as generic decisions—recommendations intended for a collection of patients rather than for a single patient.

Beyond these similarities, however, are some important differences that make practice policies considerably more difficult to design. In the case of a decision, the outcomes and preferences apply to a particular patient.

There might be a range of uncertainty about the outcomes, the comparisons might be difficult, and there will be varying degrees of conviction about which option is best, but, in theory at least, there is a single option that is best for that patient. Practice policies are inherently more difficult because they attempt to make decisions for a collection of patients. This additional dimension adds several types of complexity.

The high stakes, uncertainty, and variability introduce a new factor into the policy-making process: flexibility.

This need is addressed by having three types of practice policies according to their intended flexibility: standards, guidelines, and options.

Epstein AM. The outcomes movement—will it get us where we want to go? *N Engl J Med*. 1990;323:266-270.

Reprinted with permission of *The New England Journal of Medicine*.

The outcomes movement is well under way. The increased allotment of funds for research is real. Already greater attention is being devoted to determining the outcomes of different interventions, and this research is likely to yield insights into efficacy and rational behavior. I believe that expanding our research focus to a broader set of outcomes will reap rewards, since traditional physiologic and clinical indexes have important limitations. Understanding how different interventions affect such factors as physical and emotional function, social activity, and return to work will provide a more sensitive gauge. Developing new and more effective methods to convey such information to doctors and patients can only lead to wiser decisions. At the same time, however, we must realize that clinical research is not a new endeavor. Will the expansion of our research effort and the development and increased accessibility of larger computerized data bases lead to a revolutionary increase in our understanding? Will these changes truly be instrumental in creating a "central nervous system" for health care? Certainly they will help, but I believe our expectations should be modest.

What about guidelines? The political tide here is strong. Images of the "rogue surgeon" practicing beyond the acceptable bounds argue strongly for an aggressive approach. The proponents of guidelines would have us develop, implement, and enforce standards for a broad set of therapies now. Is that feasible? Clearly, the consensus process can provide an answer, and when the education of physicians is ineffective in changing practice, stronger administrative and financial levers can be used. But will such efforts make the provision of care more rational and lead to a more efficient system?

Fuchs VR, Garber AM. The new technology assessment. *N Engl J Med.* 1990;323:673-678.

Reprinted with permission of *The New England Journal of Medicine.*

Technology assessment is not a new phenomenon in medicine. The most able and conscientious physicians have always sought to understand the effects of the interventions they apply. With the development of clinical research, attempts to establish safety and efficacy became more systematic and scientific, culminating in the crown jewel of traditional technology assessment, the randomized clinical trial.

The most striking differences between the new and the old forms of technology assessment arise from a broadening of perspective. The old form emphasized the biomedical perspective—that is, the safety and efficacy of an intervention. The new technology assessment, with its broader perspective, is usually conducted by different researchers who apply different methods and seek different data. Because it evaluates a wider spectrum of consequences of health interventions, the new technology assessment is more challenging, more complex, more controversial, and potentially more useful than the old one.

The effects of the new technology assessment, like those of any tool, depend on the way it is used. To physicians, the new method of assessment represents both a threat and an opportunity. Government and private payers may use it to micromanage health care and interfere further with the physician-patient relationship. But it can provide physicians with critical information with which to evaluate and improve their clinical practices....The new technology assessment explicitly incorporates considerations that clinicians have long claimed are integral to making decisions about the care of individual patients—the circumstances, needs, and values unique to each. In an era when government, insurance companies, and employers insist on cost containment, the new technology assessment can be the most powerful tool physicians have to protect the interests of their patients.

Leape LL, Park RE, Solomon DH, et al. Does inappropriate use explain small-area variations in the use of health care services? *JAMA*. 1990;263:669-672.

For many years, using a variety of research designs, and under varying circumstances, investigators have reported geographic variations in the use of medical and surgical procedures. Although many explanations for these differences have been proposed, the evidence supporting them is inconclusive or conflicting. Common to most of the proposed explanations has been the untested assumption that high use rates were the result of inappropriate application (use of procedures that did not improve the patient's health or that even harmed it).

For coronary angiography, analyses based on either large- or small-area data showed a moderate relationship between rates of use and fraction of inappropriate use. For carotid endarterectomy and UGI endoscopy, no significant relationship was found, and results thus were not consistent with the hypothesis that appropriateness explains use.

Our data provide inferential evidence against several other theories that have been proposed to account for geographic variations: differences in disease incidence and local overuse or underuse of medical care in general. Differences in the incidence of disease seems less probable when variations are measured in small as opposed to large areas because neighboring counties would be expected to have similar disease rates.

Perhaps the most important implication of the study is that overuse is not simply defined by rate of use, and it is not limited to high-use areas. Overuse, which we defined as inappropriate use, of these three procedures occurred in small areas with low use rates as well as in areas with high rates.

Lohr KN, Schroeder SA. A strategy for quality assurance in Medicare. *N Engl J Med*. 1990;322:707-712.

The Institute of Medicine of the National Academy of Sciences has just released a report on quality assurance for the Medicare program. The legislation authorizing the study called for an ambitious and far-reaching strategic plan for assessing and ensuring the quality of medical care for elderly people during the next decade.

The resulting report indicates that although the current quality of medical care for Medicare enrollees is not bad, it could be improved; that the current system to assess and ensure quality is in general not very effective and may have serious unintended consequences; and that exciting opportunities are now emerging to set in place a comprehensive system of quality assurance that can address itself to improving the health of elderly people.

The committee recommended a number of steps for a strategy of quality review and assurance for Medicare. One called on Congress to expand the mission of Medicare to include an explicit responsibility for ensuring the quality of care of Medicare enrollees. Thus, any new Medicare quality-assurance program must give more attention to the processes of patient-practitioner interaction and decision making, to broad health and quality-of-life outcomes, and to patient satisfaction and well-being. Three goals for a Medicare quality-assurance program were stated: continuously improving the quality of health care for Medicare enrollees, strengthening the ability of health care organizations and practitioners to assess and improve their own performance, and identifying and overcoming systemic and policy barriers to good quality of care.

The committee's central recommendation was that Congress restructure the existing PRO [peer-review organization] program, redefine its functions, and implement a new program—the Medicare Program to Assure Quality, or MPAQ.

...the MPAQ would be explicitly oriented to quality of care, not to utilization or cost control.

Lomas J, Anderson GM, Dominick-Pierre K, et al. Do practice guidelines guide practice? N Engl J Med. 1989;321:1306-1311.

Reprinted with permission of *The New England Journal of Medicine.*

Guidelines for medical practice can contribute to improved care only if they succeed in moving actual practice closer to the behaviors the guidelines recommend. To assess the effect of such guidelines, we surveyed hospitals and obstetricians in Ontario before and after the release of a widely distributed and nationally endorsed consensus statement recommending decreases in the use of cesarean sections. These surveys, along with discharge data from hospitals reflecting actual practice, revealed that most obstetricians (87 to 94 percent) were aware of the guidelines and that most (82.5 to 85 percent) agreed with them. Attitudes toward the use of cesarean section were congruent with the recommendations even before their release. One third of the hospitals and obstetricians reported changing their practice as a consequence of the guidelines, and obstetricians reported rates of cesarean section in women with a previous cesarean section that were significantly reduced, in keeping with the recommendations (from 72.2 percent to 61.1 percent; P<0.01). The surveys also showed, however, that knowledge of the content of the recommendations was poor (67 percent correct responses). Furthermore, data on actual practice after the publication of the guidelines showed that the rates of cesarean section were 15 to 49 percent higher than the rates reported by obstetricians, and they showed only a slight change from the previous upward trend.

We conclude that guidelines for practice may predispose physicians to consider changing their behavior, but that unless there are other incentives or the removal of disincentives, guidelines may be unlikely to effect rapid change in actual practice. We believe that incentives should operate at the local level, although they may include system-wide economic changes.

Park RE, Brook RH, Kosecoff J, et al. Explaining variations in hospital death rates. *JAMA*. 1990;264:484-490.

It would be convenient if hospitals with higher death rates, identified by using easily collected administrative data (age, sex, previous hospitalization, diagnosis), turned out to be providing lower quality of care. It is easy to use administrative data to identify hospitals with high death rates. If a high death rate were a marker for bad care, then health care consumers would know to avoid those hospitals, and professional organizations and the hospitals themselves could work to correct the quality problems.

We stated our main study objectives as follows: (1) to determine if hospitals with high death rates provide lower-quality care or have more severely ill patients than do hospitals with lower death rates and (2) to determine at the patient level how the probability of death is related to severity of illness and quality of care.

With respect to the first objective, we determined that hospitals targeted with unexpectedly high age-sex-race-disease-specific-death rates do not provide lower quality of care than do untargeted hospitals, and that any differences in quality of care that lie within estimated confidence bounds have minimal effects on death rates.

With respect to the second objective, we determined that, at an individual patient level, higher severity of illness markedly increases the probability of death, and, to a lesser extent, better quality of care reduces the probability of death.

If one believes that quality differs among hospitals and that it is important to detect the differences, the more important question is whether a targeting mechanism can be devised that better identifies hospitals providing lower-quality care. For that reason, we retargeted the hospitals in our data set to take account of...possible limitations in our targeting method.

Tarlov AR, Ware JE, Greenfield S, et al. The medical outcomes study: an application of methods for monitoring the results of medical care. *JAMA*. 1989;262:925-930.

The medical care system in the United States is being restructured, with the goal of containing rising health care expenditures. Cost-containment strategies, which have included diagnosis related groups, prepaid health plans, preferred provider organizations, and professional review organizations, have as their major purpose restraining the use of high-cost medical services. Yet little attention has been paid to how patients' health and level of functioning in everyday activities are affected by these and other strategies.

The Medical Outcomes Study (MOS) was a 2-year observational study designed to help understand how specific components of the health care system affect the outcomes of care. The MOS has two purposes: (1) to relate variations in patient outcomes to differences in the system from which the patient receives care, clinician specialty training, the intensity of resource use, and clinicians' technical and interpersonal styles and (2) to develop more practical tools for monitoring patient outcomes, and their determinants, in routine practice.

The MOS is a new paradigm for monitoring the results of medical care. As such, it required a new database. We have demonstrated the feasibility of collecting the necessary data in a number of diverse practice settings in three cities. The stage is now set for us to evaluate the usefulness of this database in increasing our understanding of how health care policies affect medical management decisions and patient outcomes.

Wennberg JE, Freeman JL, Shelton RM, Bubolz TA. Hospital use and mortality among Medicare beneficiaries in Boston and New Haven. *N Engl J Med.* 1989;321:1168-1173.

Reprinted with permission of *The New England Journal of Medicine.*

We compared rates of hospital use and mortality in fiscal year 1985 among Medicare enrollees in Boston and New Haven, Connecticut.

Adjusted rates of discharge, readmission, length of stay, and reimbursement were 47, 29, 15, and 79 percent higher, respectively, in Boston; 40 percent of Boston's deaths occurred in hospitals as compared with 32 percent of New Haven's. High-variation medical conditions (those for which there is little consensus about the need for hospitalization) accounted for most of these differences. By contrast, discharge rates for low-variation medical conditions (which tend to reflect the incidence of disease) were similar. Inpatient case-fatality rates were lower in Boston than in New Haven (RR = 0.85; 95 percent confidence interval, 0.78 to 0.92), but when all deaths (regardless of place of death) were measured, the mortality rates in Boston and New Haven were nearly identical (RR = 0.99; 95 percent confidence interval, 0.93 to 1.05).

We conclude that the lower rate of hospital use by Medicare enrollees in New Haven was not associated with a higher overall mortality rate. Population-based as well as hospital-based statistics are needed to evaluate differences in hospital mortality rates for high-variation medical conditions.

COMMENTARY

Phillip M. Forman

"Quality is Job One." So says the Ford Motor Company. As a periodic consumer of automobiles, my concern for quality is almost wholly with the outcome of Ford's—or any other manufacturer's—efforts. I seek value by attempting to choose the highest quality care at the price I am prepared to pay. I can judge the quality (e.g., appearance, performance, reliability, durability) by my own assessments that are based on experience and comparisons with other vehicles. In addition, I may research the assessments of others, such as independent consumer groups. Thus, I can become an informed consumer.

However, I am unlikely—except perhaps as a citizen concerned with our nation's international competitiveness—to want to evaluate the organizational structure and the processes through which Ford may be seeking to achieve its quality goals. I am focusing on the *outcome.*

Furthermore, while my personal decisions in selecting an automobile may be aggregated with those of many others in the population, thus creating some measure of consensus on car quality and value, my errors will be largely *private.* They will only harm me and perhaps my checkbook.

Quality is now a buzzword in health care. And the current emphasis on outcomes research as a key element in the development of practice guidelines is evident from the topics in this chapter on *Quality, Outcomes, and Effectiveness of Care.* The attention to clinical outcomes and development of appropriate guidelines is overdue, welcomed, and essential.

Nevertheless, the patient, the so-called consumer of health care, differs from the car buyer in very important, fundamental ways. The organizational structure and processes of the health care industry do impact the patient, both immediately and personally. Quality of health care is not solely an issue of outcome, and patients are rightly concerned with structure and process. In addition, becoming an informed consumer of health care, if feasible at all, is far more complex and difficult than becoming an informed purchaser of an automobile. Individual patient/consumer choices can harm the public in ways now all too familiar as evidenced in the articles and reports in this publication. Indeed, achieving some semblence of consensus on what represents quality and value in health care seems very distant.

In addition to the desired outcomes of a diagnostic or therapeutic intervention, quality health care involves issues of caring, appropriateness, professional competence, efficiency, accessibility, and more. When one considers quality health care in this broad sense, it is clear that quality concerns are inseparable from those of access and cost. Thus, quality transcends its linkage to outcomes and bears upon many issues, including public dissatisfaction, financing, structure of the system, access to care, and rationing. Quality is indeed "job one."

The present priorities for health services research also tend to focus on expanded efforts to assess outcomes and develop practice guidelines. Yet, as with the larger view of quality, it is critical that we do not undervalue or lose sight of the full scope of health services research. This multidisciplinary field of inquiry addresses questions of access and costs, as well as quality within the framework of structure and process, without forgetting outcomes.

This nation's academic health centers are the most significant source of leadership and talent for strengthening health services research, thereby contributing to solving the dilemmas we face in health care today.

COMMENTARY

John Naughton

The American society, through elected representatives, patient advocacy groups, private insurance payers and other constituencies, has confirmed a perception of generalized dissatisfaction with the manner in which health and medical care are provided. Similar dissatisfaction exists within the professional provider communities, albeit from a differing perception. Although the sources of discontent are easily identifiable, the development of any single solution for a pluralistic society committed to the preservation of individual autonomy and social diversity cannot be readily achieved. Available evidence suggests that when solutions are focused on a single conclusion or approach, any solution will fail. Given the prospects that a contentious environment will exist for a protracted and indefinite period of time, the attempts to develop strategies and alternatives for remedying the problems are increasingly based on the hope that from a number of diverse approaches a more comprehensive and coordinated public policy structure will emanate through evolution rather than revolution. Whatever the approach, it is apparent that so-called policymakers, state governments and the federal government see the nation's medical schools and their defined academic health centers as important foci and catalysts for the provision of health leadership, development of new kinds of manpower, and performing as social agents through which needed strategies and policies will evolve. Such external forces, of course, create a sense of threat and instability to the academic health centers at a time when the total fabric of the structure and concept of this post-World War II institution seems under attack.

One set of strategies that evolved during the 1980s was to develop cost containment approaches that required significant behavioral changes among health care professionals and institutions involved in health and medical care. The objectives that were developed included utilization review, cost-benefit analysis of selected patient care services, technological assessment, and increased emphasis on outcomes research as opposed to the correctness of process.

The articles published in 1990 relating to quality assurance reflect the complexity and the diversity of issues and changes that came about in medical practice through the course of the current generation. A series of articles published by David M. Eddy, M.D., Ph.D., serves to focus on the issue of clinical decision making. Each of the nine articles focuses on some aspect of the decision-making process and attempts to relate how scientific evaluation of the process and its application can be translated into some form of action, which might eventuate into public policy. Eddy's initial article, *The Challenge*, focuses on the challenge of using decision analysis to influence the behavior of physicians to improve patient outcomes. He correctly emphasizes that: (1) if these important goals are to be achieved, the emphasis must be directed toward **quality** rather than to **cost containment**; (2) physicians must be involved intimately in the process; and (3) the ultimate goal must be to improve a physician's capacity to improve decision-making skills. He correctly emphasizes the basic tenets required of a good physician, that is, the ability to attain correct and critical information and to analyze it in a manner that leads to correct diagnostic interpretation. The latter, in turn, should lead to a more efficient, less cumbersome course of evaluation and intervention. However, one is reminded by many experts that unless some form of facilitation at the bedside and in the ambulatory setting occurs, Eddy's work and that of his peers could end up as no more than a "theory about theories."

Eddy's other articles detail how decisions are made; what practice policies are; from whence practice policies emanate; how ideas and actions eventuate into policy; and most importantly, the potential outcomes of the processes, namely the development of practice policies which provide the standards, guidelines and options which could determine optimal medical practice. The latter concepts should send a chill through any good educator's or physician's spine, for they tend to suggest that all that needs to be known about good medical care is known; therefore, the need and opportunity to explore new avenues of diagnosis, evaluation and intervention are no longer needed. No one can argue with the concept that for a vast number of medical and biological conditions, there is a correct way to attain the diagnosis and a limited number of acceptable ways in which to intervene. But, to assume that good medical practice and the betterment of society can be ensured by this approach represents an issue which academic leaders should debate and evaluate actively and vigorously before accepting it at face value.

By his own admission, Eddy indicates that the issues are not really about the practices of good, dedicated, competent physicians, but are about the wide variability with which physicians, individually and collectively, address what seem to be common medical conditions or ailments. Of course, this is predicated on the assumption that each so-called common problem is identical and that the physician-patient interaction is not a variable with which to contend. It seems to this writer that the concept of patient care options and patient care guidelines is an acceptable one. The concept of a rigorous form of standards of practice is one which could do great damage to the need to explore continually the causes and cures for the abnormal human condition.

Epstein reviewed the outcomes movement in a *Sounding Board* article in *The New England Journal of Medicine*. He speaks, as most of us do, for the appropriate assessment and accountability, but cautions that the use of guidelines does not ensure the provision of more rational or more cost-efficient patient care. Brook argues in favor of practice guidelines provided they are developed with the best methods available and are applied constructively. Tarlov and his colleagues reported a methodology designed to monitor the results of medical care. In this cross-sectional study, being performed in Boston, Chicago and Los Angeles, 523 physicians were randomly selected to participate. The total patient sample is 22,462 of which 2,349 patients with diabetes, hypertension, coronary heart disease, and/or depression are studied longitudinally. The actual results await analysis and publication. This approach could well serve as a model for moving this current approach to quality control and assessment forward.

Brook, together with his colleagues, reported on aspects of the quality of patient care in the ambulatory setting. The group studies both process and outcome of care in 5,986 adults below age 65 and children below age 14 years. The cohort had 17 different chronic conditions. While the results were not definitive, the study indicated that quality of care and compliance with therapeutic regimens were higher in patients enrolled in free insurance plans compared to those which required cost sharing. There was a deficiency both in meeting outcome and process criteria. Of the patients interviewed by physicians at the end of the study, there was a feeling that treatment could be altered in 70 percent of the group, but that any change in the regimen would benefit only 30 percent of that subset of patients. The authors concluded that this study could form one model for evolutionary means of testing quality of care and its outcomes.

The interest and concern for improved quality at an appropriate cost has stimulated the development of the Agency for Health Care Policy and Research, a new agency within the U.S. Department of Health and Human Services that will award peer reviewed grants directed at determining the effectiveness of care and various interventions. The authorized allocation for fiscal '91 is $100 million. The definitions of technology assessments and the implications for the practice of medicine are well described in a *Sounding Board* article in *The New England Journal of Medicine* by Fuchs and Garber.

Other articles deal with clinical evaluations of quality of care. The study by Lomas and his colleagues concerns the effectiveness of practice guidelines in changing physician behavior in Canada. The guidelines promulgated related to the use of cesarean sections. These authors reported that a statistically significant reduction in repeat cesarean sections occurred following the release of the guidelines. However, first time sections continued to increase. While the vast majority of obstetricians were familiar with the release of such guidelines and supportive of them, far fewer actually read them or were familiar with their contents.

The Wennberg article compared hospital use and mortality rates among Medicare recipients in Boston and New Haven. While these are two Eastern cities with strong medical school-teaching hospital influences, it was interesting to observe that Boston was an apparent over-utilizer of services compared to New Haven. The over-utilization in Boston is probably related to an excess capacity of acute care beds, a situation which permits admitting less severely-ill patients and patients with essentially non-debilitating illnesses to hospitals with increased frequency. The end result, of course, is that per unit costs are higher in Boston than New Haven. While one could obviously argue that New Haven might benefit from an increase in acute care bed capacity, the concept is muted by the fact that overall community mortality rates for Medicare beneficiaries did not differ between Boston and New Haven. This outcome indicates that hospitalization for many of the patients in Boston was unnecessary, and that the required care could have been rendered at lower costs to the Medicare program in other environments.

Park argues strongly against using simplified approaches to detect the reasons for variations in death rates among hospitals. They studied 1,126 patients with congestive heart failure and 1,150 patients with myocardial infarction using Medicare (Part A) administrative data. The investigators compared those hospitals in four states with higher than expected mortality rates with those with lower than average mortality. Using their techniques they were not able to account for the differences in mortality based on the process of care. They concluded that more than administrative data is required to evaluate mortality and a time span of more than one year is also probably required.

The published articles for 1990 suggest that changes in quality assurance, improved patient care, and cost effectiveness will come through voluntary action by the medical profession under the stimulus of government and private insurance payers and other societal constituents. While this is the desirable outcome, the experience in New York

State has differed considerably from that approach. Legislative and legal remedies have been invoked which place the responsibility for protecting the patient's well-being under the regulatory process. The Malpractice Reform Act of 1985[1] and a grand jury indictment in the now famous Libby Zion[2] case led to accelerated reform in quality assurance and in graduate medical education. The act places the responsibility for patient care directly on each hospital's board of trustees, thus elevating the responsibility solely from the medical staffs to involvement by lay and professional people. It is the perception of most people that this approach has been buttressed primarily by disincentives rather than incentives.

The jury is still out as to the benefits of these changes, but there is the distinct impression that the emphasis on quality of care by physicians and medical educators has improved. However, concerns by lay persons who must be willing to assume these awesome responsibilities could make it less attractive to become a hospital board member. Clearly many physicians have found themselves practicing in an environment of increased anxiety and concern, a situation which tends to reduce their confidence and morale. For proponents of voluntary change, the New York experience is a warning to the wise that hesitation and procrastination are inappropriate mechanisms to employ at this time of rapid change in health care.

The Libby Zion case occurred coincidentally in a temporal sequence with the development of the malpractice reform act. The Zion case was referred to a grand jury. Although indictments against the physicians and hospital involved in her care and death were not forthcoming, the grand jury did demand that New York State through the state department of health initiate significant reform in graduate medical education. The Bell Commission took the mandate and proceeded to modify Code 405 to introduce required credentialing of residents and a reduction in working hours. These changes were accompanied by an increased cost for health care because of the need to replace resident services with that provided by other health professionals. New York State is now considered a leader in both medical education and health care reform having placed tremendous emphasis on outcomes as opposed to process of care.

REFERENCES

1. State of New York: Official compilation of guides, rules and regulation. Albany, New York: Lenz and Riecker, Inc.
2. Sullivan R. Grand jury assails hospital in '84 death of 18-year-old. *New York Times*, B3, January 13, 1987.

CHAPTER VIII

Financing of Health Care and Physician Payment Reform

ABSTRACTS AND EXCERPTS

Epstein AM, Stern RS, Weissman JS. Do the poor cost more? A multihospital study of patients' socioeconomic status and use of hospital resources. *N Engl J Med.* 1990;322:1122-1128.

Reprinted with permission of *The New England Journal of Medicine.*

There is controversy about whether hospitalized poor patients use more resources and whether hospitals that provide care for the poor therefore merit supplementary payment under per-case prospective payment systems. We previously reported that patients of low socioeconomic status with connective-tissue disease had longer hospital stays and higher costs than patients of higher socioeconomic status at a single hospital. To examine the generalizability of this phenomenon, we interviewed 16,903 (83 percent) of 20,278 consecutive adult patients (excluding obstetrical and psychiatric patients) admitted in 1987 to five Massachusetts hospitals, to obtain information on three direct measures of socioeconomic status (income, occupation, and education). We divided each measure into three strata. Thus, there were 15 comparisons—three measures of socioeconomic status applied to each of five hospitals.

After excluding outliers and adjusting for diagnosis-related group (DRG), we found that the patients of the lowest socioeconomic status had hospital stays 3 to 30 percent longer than those of patients of higher status, the differences varying with the hospital and the indicator of socioeconomic status (P ≤ 0.05 for 11 of the 15 comparisons). Hospital charges were 1 to 18 percent higher for the patients of lowest socioeconomic status than for those of higher status (P ≤ 0.05 for 9 of 15 comparisons). When we adjusted for age, severity of illness, and DRG, the patients of lowest socioeconomic status had longer stays than those of higher status in 14 of 15 comparisons (P < 0.05 for 7 of the 15) and higher charges in 13 of 15 comparisons (P, 0.05 for 6 of the 15). The differences between patients of high and low status ranged up to 21 percent for length of stay and 13 percent for charges.

Our findings suggest that hospitalized patients of lower socioeconomic status have longer stays and probably require more resources. Supplementary payments to hospitals for the treatment of poor patients merit further consideration.

Freund DA, Rossiter LF, Fox PD, et al. Evaluation of the Medicaid competition demonstrations. *Health Care Financing Review* 1989;11:81-87.

In 1983, the Health Care Financing Administration funded a multiyear evaluation of Medicaid demonstrations in six States. The alternative delivery systems represented by the demonstrations contained a number of innovative features, most notably capitation, case management, limitations on provider choice, and provider competition. Implementation and operation issues as well as demonstration effects on utilization and cost of care, administrative costs, rate setting, biased selection, quality of care, and access and satisfaction were evaluated.

The evaluation of the demonstrations provided a detailed understanding of the implementation and operation of the programs, as well as a comprehensive assessment of program features of case management, capitation, limitation on freedom of choice, and competition on several outcome measures across several program designs. Although much has changed in the Medicaid program since these demonstrations were conceived in the early 1980s, a number of important findings with policy and managerial significance were revealed.

Primary care case-management responsibility produced significant effects on service delivery patterns, in particular emergency room use, for virtually all of the programs.

Despite the reductions in utilization, however, first-year program expenditures were not substantially reduced for any of the demonstrations. This lack of cost savings in the first demonstration year is primarily the result of very limited reductions in inpatient use and of the basing of capitation rates on prior-year use levels....capitation provides the opportunity to develop greater predictability and control in program expenditures and provides a buffer against rapid cost changes in the future.

The limitation on freedom of choice of provider that accompanied case management and capitation did not have an adverse effect on quality of care, as measured through in-office medical record abstraction of tracer conditions indicative of process and outcome.

...no insurmountable problems were encountered by the demonstrations in accomplishing full enrollment of Medicaid beneficiaries. It appears practical to expect that the Medicaid population will enroll in prepaid plans.

The Medicaid population often is reported to have difficulty accessing what is an apparently fragmented fee-for-service system. The results from this evaluation provide some indication of the promise of prepaid case management to better organize the caregiving, to reduce unnecessary service use, and to match the quality of care obtained in traditional fee-for-service Medicaid.

Ginsburg PB, LeRoy LB, Hammons GT. Medicare physician payment reform. *Health Aff.* 1990;9:178-188.

Reprinted with permission of *Health Affairs.*

On November 21, 1989, the 101st Congress passed legislation that established a comprehensive reform of Medicare physician payment. The reform included a fee schedule based on resource costs, limits on physicians' balance billing, Medicare volume performance standards (MVPS), and increased support of effectiveness research and practice guidelines. The legislation followed closely the recommendations of the Physician Payment Review Commission (PPRC), and entity of Congress that was created in 1986 to advise it on these issues.

While some have labeled the reform provisions as "revolutionary," many aspects of the policy are logical extensions of policy changes enacted over the past five years. For example, departures from charge-based relative values began in 1986 with reductions in payment for cataract surgery. Restrictions on physician charges began in 1984 when charges were frozen along with Medicare payments. Basing fee updates on comparisons of expenditure increases with what is judged affordable has been pursued since 1984. A number of specialty societies have developed and disseminated practice guidelines. The payment reform policy builds on these relatively fragmented policy efforts by combining them and pursuing them with greater determination and purpose.

Implementation of these policies over the next few years will require the efforts of many and require further policy decisions.

While the commitment to providing physicians more information on appropriateness and effectiveness is clear, researchers and clinicians have much work to do to change clinical practice. Support by the medical profession will be critical to success in this area.

Goldsmith J. A radical prescription for hospitals. *Harvard Bus Rev.* 1989; May-June:104-111.

Hospitals face a grim short-term prognosis. After moderating in the 1984 to 1986 period, health costs are soaring again. Health insurance premium increases of 20% to 40% have prompted employers to renew their scrutiny of benefit costs. Congress and the Bush administration, looking for ways to pare the huge budget deficit, seem likely to take the knife to Medicare, hospitals' largest payment source. The unrelenting economic pressure on hospitals may finally produce the long-predicted closure of the 700 to 1,000 institutions in deepest trouble.

While the short-term outlook is not promising, the long-term view is in a sense very favorable. Except for major regional institutions, the acute-care hospital as we know it will probably not survive. The successful hospital of the future will be a far different institution that focuses on early diagnosis and management of chronic illness. The hospital of the future will reach out into homes and residential communities as much as it depends on the sick to cross its threshold for help. This is the radical prescription in store for hospitals.

As cost constraints get tighter and tighter, managing in a world of scarce resources without damaging the quality of patient care becomes a more pressing issue.

...most illness will be associated with the infirmities of aging. The community hospital will decentralize its services and weave them into the fabric of the neighborhood and the community. The main role of most community hospitals will be diagnosis and treatment of the chronically ill.

Hillman AL, Pauly MV, Kerstein JJ. How do financial incentives affect physicians' clinical decisions and the financial performance of health maintenance organizations? *N Engl J Med.* 1989;321:86-92.

Reprinted with permission of *The New England Journal of Medicine.*

It has been suggested that the use of financial incentives by health maintenance organizations (HMOs) may change physicians' behavior toward individual patients. To test this hypothesis, we used a regression analysis of data from a survey of HMOs to examine the relation between the presence of financial incentives and two measures of the use of resources (the rate of hospitalization and the rate of visits for outpatient services) and one measure of the HMOs' financial viability (the achievement of break-even status). When we controlled for the effect of market-area variables, we found that some forms of compensation were significantly associated with these indicators of decision making by physicians.

Among methods of paying physicians, the use of capitation or salaries was associated with a lower rate of hospitalization than the use of fee-of-service payment; physicians in for-profit HMOs and group-model HMOs also used the hospital less often. Placing physicians at financial risk as individuals and imposing penalties for deficits in the HMO's hospital fund beyond the loss of withheld funds were associated with fewer outpatient visits per enrollee, but a higher percentage of HMO patients in a physician's caseload was associated with more frequent visits. HMOs were more likely to break even if they were larger, older, had physicians at personal financial risk for the cost of outpatient tests; break-even status was also related to the type of HMO.

We conclude that the use of some, but not all, financial incentives, as well as the type of HMO, does influence the behavior of physicians toward patients. It remains to be determined how these factors affect the quality of care.

Hsiao WC, Braun P, Becker ER, et al. A national study of resource-based relative value scales for physician services: phase II. (HCFA Contract No. 17-C298795/1-03) 1990.

The Federal Government, organized medicine, physicians and patients all agree that the customary, prevailing and reasonable (CPR) method of payment that is currently used to pay for physician services is complex, inflationary and inequitable. In response to these deficiencies in the current system, Congress enacted a comprehensive law in December 1989 to reform Medicare physician payments. The law contains three major elements.

First, the current CPR payment mechanism will be replaced by a fee schedule for physician services based on a resource-based relative value scale (RBRVS). The RBRVS includes three major components of resource costs that are required for physician services: physician's work, practice expenses and the cost of professional liability insurance. The national uniform relative values will be adjusted for each locality by geographic adjustment factors (GAF). Second, the law also establishes a Medicare volume performance standard that sets a target rate of increase for expenditures for Medicare physician services. Last, beneficiaries will be protected from excessive balance billing by physicians; eventually, the additional amount that nonparticipating physicians can charge Medicare patients will be limited to 15 percent of the Medicare fee paid to nonparticipating physicians.

The key building block for the Medicare Fee Schedule is the RBRVS which was developed by the Harvard researchers between 1986 and 1988, with funding from HCFA. The methods, data and results of the study were published in September 1988 and were carefully reviewed by HCFA, PPRC, organized medicine and academic researchers. The numerous reviews found, in general, that the RBRVS based on physician's work input can be developed, that a common relative value scale can be established across all specialties, and that the relative values derived are reliable and have validity.

A major limitation of the RBRVS is that it considers only the cost of the resource input required to perform a service. Meanwhile, the quality of service varies between physicians and social benefits vary between services. These elements have not been considered in the RBRVS-based Medicare Fee Schedule.

The Federal Government has mounted a major effort to develop clinical guidelines to determine the appropriateness of care. To the extent that these guidelines define appropriate care, they may also approximate standards for quality of care. In order for the clinical guidelines to be successful, the incentive structure must be integrated with it so that physicians are given compensation for practicing appropriately. Otherwise, the program for appropriateness of care will have to rely strictly on regulation to affect physicians' practices. Monitoring and controlling physicians practices is cumbersome, difficult, expensive and often counterproductive. A more voluntary and decentralized approach that incorporates the proper incentives in the Medicare Fee Schedule may be more successful in promoting appropriate medical practice and in reducing costs. The research that would align the RBRVS with the appropriateness of care remains to be done.

Lee PR, Ginsburg PB, LeRoy LB, Hammons GT, et al. The Physician Payment Review Commission Report to Congress. *JAMA*. 1989;261:2382-2385.

To rationalize the pattern of payments by Medicare, the Commission proposes a Medicare Fee Schedule based primarily on resource costs. To limit beneficiary financial liability, it recommends limits on balance billing. To control growth in expenditures, the Commission proposes the use of expenditure targets of medical services, and development of practice guidelines.

The Commission recommends that Congress enact legislation this year that would replace Medicare's current "customary, prevailing, and reasonable" method of paying physicians with a fee schedule based primarily on resource costs.

A fee schedule consists of:

- a relative value scale (RVS), which indicates the value of each service or procedure relative to others;
- a conversion factor, which translates the RVS into a fee for each service; and

- a geographic multiplier, which indicates how payment for a service is to vary from one geographic area to another.

The Commission recommends that the geographic multiplier reflect only variation in overhead costs of practice. The amount physicians receive for their time and effort, after subtracting overhead costs, should not vary by locality. Therefore, if physicians in two parts of the country provide the same quantity and mix of services to Medicare beneficiaries, they would receive the same net income from Medicare. This policy would reduce substantially the magnitude of geographic variation in fees.

Reducing inappropriate and unnecessary services is the best way to contain costs while not sacrificing access and quality of care.

The Commission recommends three approaches to slowing expenditure growth as follows:
- giving physicians collective incentives to contain costs through expenditure targets,
- increasing research on effectiveness of care and expanding the development and dissemination of practice guidelines, and
- improving utilization management by carriers and peer review organizations.

Expenditure targets will help slow the increase in Medicare expenditures so that we as a society can meet other pressing social needs. And increased effectiveness research and practice guidelines will provide us with the knowledge and means to manage available health care resources more wisely.

Levy JM, Borowitz MJ, Jencks SF, et al. Impact of the Medicare fee schedule on payments to physicians. *JAMA.* 1990;264:717-722.

Beginning in 1992, the Medicare program will pay physicians by the Medicare Fee Schedule, a system of geographically adjusted standardized payment rates based in part on the Resource-Based Relative Value Scale developed by Hsaio et al and in part on current Medicare payments. In our simulations of the Medicare Fee Schedule, we find that (1) redistributions of Medicare-allowed charges across specialties will be substantial but approximately only half the size projected by Hsaio, (2) there will be large redistributions among geographic areas that tend to compound the specialty redistributions, and (3) there will be wide variation within specialties as to how individual providers are affected. The majority of the redistributive impact of the Medicare Fee Schedule is attributable to implementation of a geographically adjusted system of standardized payments rather than to the particular work values developed by Hsiao et al in the Resource-Based Relative Value Scale.

Munoz E, Rosner F, Chalfin D, et al. Age, resource consumption, and outcome for medical patients at an academic medical center. *Arch Intern Med.* 1989; 149:1946-1950.

The federal DRG hospital payment system has had no major changes since its inception 6 years ago. We studied all medical admissions to a large academic medical center for a 3-year period and demonstrated that older medical patients had (on average) higher total hospital costs, longer hospital lengths of stay, and a greater mortality than younger medical patients. Older medical patients had more diagnoses per patient and demonstrated higher rates of emergency and intensive care unit admissions, as well as a greater need for blood transfusions. Older medical patients also would have generated significant financial risk to our hospital under DRG reimbursement for all patients (especially patients aged 71 years or older). These findings suggest that the current DRG classification system may be inequitable vis-á-vis the older medical patient and that medical DRGs should be further stratified regarding resource consumption to assure access and quality of care for elderly medical patients.

Tierney WM, Miller ME, McDonald CJ. The effect on test ordering of informing physicians of the charges for outpatient diagnostic tests. *N Engl J Med.* 1990;322:1499-1504.

A number of strategies have been used in an attempt to reduce diagnostic testing. The most successful—systematic monitoring of tests ordered, with criticism by senior physicians—reduced testing by up to 30 percent. These are time-consuming and expensive, however, and their use was not continued after the studies ended.

Since 1984, physicians in our academic general medical practice have ordered all outpatient diagnostic tests through a network of microcomputer workstations. The display of specific information about the patient on the computer screen has reduced the number of outpatient tests ordered and the resulting charges by 8 to 18 percent; the reductions occurred primarily in the ordering of tests with a low yield of abnormal results. Because physicians are often unaware of the costs of diagnostic tests, we hypothesized that physicians would order fewer tests if, when they ordered tests, they were reminded of the charges. We tested this hypothesis in a randomized, controlled trial.

We found that physicians ordered fewer diagnostic tests when they were given information about the charges for tests during the test-ordering process. The resulting reduction in charges to the patient or insurer was almost $7 per patient visit; if extrapolated to our entire primary care practice, this change would reduce total charges by more than $250,000 annually. The effect was greater for scheduled visits, when the physicians' habits and practice patterns may be the main factors in the decision to order tests, than for unscheduled visits, when the patients' symptoms and clinical condition may dominate decisions about testing.

COMMENTARY

Judith A. Cooksey

C oncerns over rising health care costs and the difficulties of controlling such costs have led Congress to initiate reform of Medicare payments to hospitals and physicians. In 1983, Medicare changed hospital payments from cost-based reimbursement to a prospective payment rate based on diagnosis related groups or DRGs. In 1992, Medicare will change physician payments from a customary, prevailing, and reasonable rate schedule to a standardized schedule derived from a resource-based relative value scale (RBRVS).

Several articles in this chapter describe the new physician payment system. The Medicare physician's fee schedule, which is a modification of the original scheme of Harvard's William Hsiao, will establish payments based on relative values for physician work, overhead and malpractice costs. The original Hsiao plan called for payment differentials for specialists (based on longer training periods and opportunity costs). However, Congress, on the advice of the Physician Payment Review Commission, rejected this notion.

Analysts have attempted to estimate the impact of this reform on physician payments. Payments are expected to increase for 'cognitive' services (evaluation and management) and to decrease for procedural services. Procedural and hospital-based specialties (surgery, ophthalmology, radiology, pathology) are expected to experience losses in payments, and the primary care specialties (family practice, internal medicine) will gain. There will be geographic variations, and modest gains in rural practices are expected.

The new system has a self-regulating factor (volume performance standards) that will be used to control costs. Payments per service will be reduced through formula for any growth in the volume of services beyond published standards. Congress has learned from the DRG experience that expected savings can be negated by creative responses of hospital providers, including DRG creep in coding, readmissions, and unbundling hospital services to the ambulatory setting. The new regulations also limit the ability of physicians who do not accept assignment to bill patients for differences between the Medicare fee and their usual charges.

Both of the Medicare payment reform plans were approved by Congress after substantial study and development by health services researchers at academic centers (Yale University for the DRG system and Harvard University for the Medicare fee schedule). In 1989 Congress recognized the need for expanded research and demonstration projects on medical effectiveness and practice guidelines and authorized the establishment of a new agency, the Agency for Health Care Policy and Research (AHCPR). It is hoped that through expanded research, demonstration projects, and dissemination of information more efficient and equitable methods and policies for financing health care services can be developed.

In the last year several studies on the factors that influence the costs of providing health care services have been published. These studies will take on increasing importance as Congress and private payers try to understand controllable factors in health care costs.

The study by Munoz identifies the age of the patient as a significant contributor to the length and stay and cost among 30,000 patients hospitalized on a medical service at a teaching hospital in New York. For patients older than 25, there was a progressive increase in length of stay and costs for each additional 10 years of age. Although private insurers have been slow in adopting the Medicare DRG system, this study would suggest that age should be considered in any expansion of the system.

The study by Epstein identifies socioeconomic status of the patient as another factor that contributes to hospital length of stay and cost among 16,000 adults hospitalized at five hospitals in Massachusetts. Lower socioeconomic status (measured by income, occupation, and education) was associated with longer hospital stays and higher cost with overall differences of 5 to 25 percent. These differences declined but persisted after correction for age and severity of illness. This study supports the Medicare policy of supplemental payments for hospitals treating higher numbers of patients of low socioeconomic status.

Since physicians control much of health care spending, studies that attempt to understand physician decision making regarding resource utilization are of critical importance. The study by Tierney examines the effect of informing physicians of the costs of diagnostic tests in an ambulatory clinic associated with an Indiana teaching hospital. They found that providing this information at the time of test ordering reduced overall test utilization and costs by about 14 percent. Since diagnostic testing is considered discretionary and a significant contributor to overall health care costs, the effect of this relatively simple intervention is noteworthy.

The study by Hillman attempts to examine the effects of financial incentives on HMO physicians' decisions to hospitalize patients or schedule outpatient visits based on a survey of over 300 HMOs. Through analysis of two regression models, these investigators tried to assess which identified physician financial variables (salary, capitation, bonus, and a variety of financial risks) and which HMO descriptors (type of HMO practice, HMO size and age) affected the rates of hospitalization and visits. They found that HMOs that paid physicians through capitation or salaries had lower rates of hospitalization than those that used fee-for-service payment. The model, which included the physician incentive and HMO descriptors, explained 15 percent of the variation in hospitalization rate; adding market-area variables explained over 40 percent of the variation. This type of study should be interpreted with caution because of the many confounding factors which affect HMO hospitalization rates, including area variations, selection bias by HMO enrollees, and the effectiveness of utilization review programs.

The study by Freund is an evaluation of six state Medicaid demonstration projects that were established in the mid-1980s to test managed care and capitation systems for Medicaid clients. The Medicaid system has problems with relatively high utilization rates and limited access to physician providers due to low reimbursement rates. These demonstration programs used case management principles to coordinate care and control utilization. The major findings were that the demonstration projects took substantial time to be established and that start up costs and administrative complexities were greater than anticipated. Overall savings after the first year were seen in decreased utilization of emergency room services with no significant cost impact, although further study time was recommended. The authors conclude that the programs offer some promise that managed care can be a workable alternative to fee-for-service payment for Medicaid beneficiaries. These programs may allow greater predictability and management of costs without significant adverse effects on quality, access, or satisfaction of clients.

R eform in physician payments has been in process during the past several decades. In the mid-1970s the American Society of Internal Medicine (ASIM) took the initiative to recommend improved reimbursement for cognitive services. ASIM was among the groups that strongly supported the development of a relative value scale for physician fees, including the Harvard study, *Resource-Based Relative Value Scale (RBRVS)*, by William C. Hsiao, Ph.D., of the department of health policy and management of Harvard University's School of Public Health.

From the beginning the basic concept of the RBRVS and physicians' participation to determine their own relative values have been controversial. It became clear early on that relative values for some services would be less than they are now and values for other services would be greater. Hsiao's studies have attempted to produce objective information for all physicians' services and have concluded that many of the primary care services have been undervalued and some invasive and surgical procedures have been overvalued.

It is unclear what the effects of the RBRVS will be when they are implemented. The Health Care Financing Administration (HCFA) anticipates that when fees are reduced by way of the RBRVS, the volume of services will increase. There is no direct objective evidence to support or refute that assumption. HCFA believes that such an increase in the volume of services will result in continued increases in the cost of health care. To offset this potential occurrence, HCFA has proposed or implemented a number of strategies such as volume control, expenditure targets, Medicare volume performance standards (MVPS), and practice guidelines to hold down the costs of medical services.

Proponents of RBRVS have consistently maintained that RBRVS alone will not reduce or hold down costs, but coupled with guidelines for practice, they can be effective. A number of practice parameters (guidelines) are now being planned and developed. The concept of parameters is supported by major medical organizations, including the American Medical Association, ASIM, the American College of Physicians and the American Academy of Family Physicians. Guidelines are to assist physicians in determining the appropriateness of a given service for a specific diagnosis. Thus, RBRVS may be viewed as a tool for determining the unit price and practice parameters as a method to reduce service utilization (volume).

The combination of price and volume guidelines may be an effective method to assist in controlling costs. It is not totally clear if such an approach will influence quality. Although the data are not available to determine the outcome, it seems unlikely that quality should necessarily be affected merely because of reimbursement. However, it becomes important to monitor inpatient and outpatient outcomes very closely to determine the effects that such changes might have on patient care.

Medical education programs should also be closely monitored to determine whether RBRVS and practice parameters influence residency selection. Most important, it may be that changes in reimbursement will improve recruitment of physicians for future careers in primary care. It is also unknown whether or not guidelines will be used by residents in training as a major part of their educational process. Some observers worry that guidelines could be used in limited ways as "cookbook" medicine and detract from the educational process in academic health centers. This, too, will require close monitoring.

If the RBRVS physician payment reform results in a major increase in primary care service fees, as appears likely, I believe medical students will be influenced to enter primary care programs. In addition, the RBRVS and practice parameters can effectively redirect the future costs of health care. There is not yet sufficient evidence to determine whether or not such changes will influence the quality of health care.

CHAPTER IX

Access to Health Care for Special Populations

ABSTRACTS AND EXCERPTS

Brown LD. The medically uninsured: problems, policies, and politics. *J Health Polit Policy Law.* **1990;15:413-426.**

The United States has the disturbing distinction that it, alone among Western democracies, permits a sizable percentage of its population to go entirely without health insurance coverage. Over the 1980s both the scope of the problem and national attention to it grew substantially. As the 1990s arrive, however, no solution appears to be imminent or even dimly visible on the horizon.

Even if markets, mandates, and Medicaid worked reasonably well as solutions for the uninsured, enough citizens would probably fall between the programmatic cracks to justify the continuation (or creation) of bad debt and charity care pools, uncompensated care trust funds, and the like, which use rate-setting and other state-run mechanisms to subsidize hospitals hit hardest by losses on the uncovered.

Major policy change in the United States usually presupposes the fulfill-ment and convergence of three conditions. First, there must be a call to arms, a widespread sense among policy leaders that an urgent (not merely ominous or impending) social problem cries out for solution. Second, policymakers must conclude that the usual ports of first call—the market, the voluntary sector, and the professions—are not up to the job and that a governmental role in problem solving is necessary. Third, policymakers must agree on a strategic model that promises to achieve desired goals without generating unacceptable side effects. Action may fail for any or all of these three reasons—because the problem at hand is not grave enough, because the market (or other nongovernmental sectors) are thought to be plausible problem-solving instruments, or because policymakers, though prepared and committed to act, cannot decide what it makes sense to do.

In the politics of the uninsured, these three conditions have not converged. Indeed, none of the three now comes close to being met....Consensus on a strategic model, and coalition building around it, are impeded by the usual proliferation of preferred solutions and the absence of structural mechanisms that would discourage proponents from falling out among themselves if a political window of opportunity were to open.

Friedman E. Medicare and Medicaid at 25. *Hospitals.* 1990;64:38-54.

Reprinted from *Hospitals*, vol. 64, no. 15, by permission, August 5, 1990, Copyright 1990, American Hospital Publishing, Inc.

Much has been written about the built-in defects of Medicare and Medicaid. Separating Medicare, which covered the politically powerful elderly, from Medicaid, which covered only a portion of several politically weak constituencies, drove a wedge between beneficiary groups that continues to cause problems today. Medicare was a national entitlement with national standards. Medicaid was a state-level entitlement, which led to patchwork coverage that was all over the map in terms of services, eligibility, and payment. Medicaid was means-tested; Medicare was not.

Through the years, quality oversight in the form of professional standards review organizations and peer review organizations was mandated; health planning through the much-despised health systems agencies came and went; hospital payment was massively reconfigured in 1983; and last year the guns of change were aimed at physicians, with the passage of a mandate for payment based on a resource-based relative value scale by 1992.

Two major factors in the history of Medicare and Medicaid—cost and data—led in the 1980s to the emergence of a third: trying to define the quality of health care in a scientific way. This revolution is really only beginning; it was kicked off largely by the introduction of Medicare prospective payment in 1983 and providers' concerns, expressed loudly, that expected cuts in payment would harm the quality of care.

In equating high cost with high quality for so long, providers may well have framed the argument in the wrong terms and led payers to lean too far in the other direction. It may take some time to correct the equation.

On their 25th anniversary, Medicare and Medicaid continue to control health policy, to determine the direction of health spending, and to hold the fate of American health care in their sometimes shaky hands.

Harvey B. Toward a national child health policy. *JAMA.* 1990; 264:252-253.

Child health objectives should be organized into a comprehensive, measurable, integrated, and feasible set of goals within a national policy. Such goals could be evaluated and prioritized in an ongoing manner so that periodic revision of resource allocation could be guided by progress toward individual goals. A major goal would be financial access to care for all children, the cornerstone of a national child health policy. Incrementalism— gradual expansion of Medicaid eligibility and expansion of employer-mandated insurance—is not likely to solve our child health problems. Medicaid, as initially envisioned, was a bold attempt to gain access to health care for the poor, but limited benefits, state variability, low reimbursement rates, and inadequate systems for providing care indicate the need for a new approach. Because of high administrative costs and lack of cost control, small employers are resistant to coverage for both employees and their dependents.

Consequently, the American Academy of Pediatrics has developed a plan to provide financial access to care for all children through age 21 years and for pregnant women. Mandated benefits would be provided either through employer-based insurance or through private insurance contracted for by states.

Mayster V, Waitzkin H, Hubbell FA, Rucker L. Local advocacy for the medically indigent. *JAMA*. 1990; 263:262-268.

Herein, we present the strategies that a countywide coalition used to improve access to services for the medically indigent. While our work has taken place in a single county with some unique characteristics, we believe that similar advocacy techniques may prove useful in other localities as well.

Local advocacy concerning indigent health care in our county has led to modest improvements in programs. Increased access, less restrictive eligibility determination, and additional funding for prenatal care and community clinics have expanded available services. Without the work of health advocates, proposed cuts in local services would surely have been deeper and more devastating. We perceive that our efforts have been effective to the extent that we have been able to coordinate several strategies: generating meaningful data, developing a politically active coalition of community advocates, and pursuing legal options.

Each of our strategies has revealed both strengths and weaknesses. Research to document local barriers to care can attract wide attention in a specific area and can affect policy decisions, yet such research involves technical compromises that limit its generalizability or pertinence in other localities. Political activism that targets the policies of county government and local health care institutions can succeed in improving access to services, but these time-consuming and largely defensive efforts do not lead to more creative or proactive programs. Although legal work can assist specific clients to obtain needed care, the litigation required to improve services for larger groups of patients, for instance the undocumented, becomes difficult to pursue.

Patton LT. Setting the rural health services research agenda: the congressional perspective. *Health Serv Res.* 1989;23:1005-1051.

After being relegated to the periphery of health policymaking for the better part of a decade, rural health care is once again a major focus of congressional concern. This resurgence of interest in rural health is reflected in almost every aspect of congressional activity. In the 100th Congress that just ended, rural health care was the subject of a record number of speeches, press releases, committee hearings, and legislation that was introduced and enacted into law. In fact, the congressionally mandated Rural Health Services Research Agenda conference, for which this article was prepared, was cited by many congressional staff as just one more reflection of the growing importance of rural health issues on Capitol Hill.

Given the continued pressure to reduce the deficit, what accounts then for the renewed interest in rural health? ...the answer lies in a confluence of developments: most notably, the deterioration of the rural economy, the introduction of Medicare's prospective payment system for hospitals, and renewed congressional concern with issues of access.

First, the rapid deterioration of the rural economy since the late 1970s has broadened congressional support for rural initiatives far beyond the traditional farm-state coalition.

Second, shortly after enactment, Medicare's prospective payment system (PPS) proved to be an explosive political catalyst for rural hospitals. With its two-tier payment system, PPS fostered the perception among rural hospital administrators that their institutions were being treated as second-class facilities—for rural advocates, PPS quickly became a metaphor for the federal government's insensitivity to rural needs.

Third, most congressional staff have felt that increased attention to rural health care has come about through the renewed congressional concern with issues of access to health care. A range of policy issues—PPS, the uninsured, malpractice, the farm crisis—have underscored the continuing shortage of rural health care facilities and personnel as well as the fact that rural residents on average are poorer, older, and less well insured than urban residents.

...rural advocates have only begun to broaden their own agenda beyond a narrow range of Medicare reimbursement issues. A more comprehensive congressional rural health agenda is still in the making.

Rowland D, Lyons B. Triple jeopardy: rural, poor, and uninsured. *Health Serv Res.* 1989;23:975-1004.

This article reviews the existing literature on urban and rural differences for the uninsured population and presents new analyses to supplement earlier research to identify issues for future research. The extent of poverty in urban and rural areas and the scope of insurance coverage for the nonelderly population is discussed in the first section on financing medical care. The second section, which covers obtaining medical care, assesses and contrasts health status and use of health services by the poor and uninsured in urban and rural areas. The final section proposes an agenda for future research.

Our current knowledge on the combined effect of poverty, lack of insurance, and rural residence is limited. Additional research to examine the influence of these factors on health status and access to care would be an important contribution to our understanding of the health effects of rural poverty. It is especially important to determine if residence in a rural area compounds the problems of poverty and lack of insurance. Some results indicate that these latter two factors are more significant than rural residence, but future research should explore the interaction of all three factors.

More extensive research on the rural population's access to care, adjusting for differences in health status as well as income and insurance status, should be undertaken. Based on the current examination, rural residents appear to see physicians at comparable rates to urban residents, but such findings need to be further disaggregated to control for differences in provider availability and site of care, and patient income, health status, and insurance coverage.

Russell L. Proposed: a comprehensive health care system for the poor. *Brookings Review*. 1989;8:13-20.

Reprinted with permission of The Brookings Institution.

What I propose is a unified, uniform, comprehensive program that would provide health care directly to the poor. Everyone with a family income below the federal poverty line would be entitled to care through this system. The eligibility criteria would be the same for everyone, everywhere in the country, and everyone would be entitled to the same benefits. All providers would be identified by the same name and logo throughout the country. The system would supply comprehensive medical services, including doctors' services, hospital care, and prescription drugs.

The proposed program would be a joint federal-state system, with the framework established by federal legislation, administration carried out by the states, and financing provided by both. Care would be given in existing government hospitals and clinics—federal, state, and local—or in hospitals and clinics under contract to government. The program would unify the structure that already serves the poor, rather than adding another piece to the current patchwork system. Financing would proceed in the same way, first combining the resources already being used for the poor, and then adding as necessary. My estimates indicate that $6 billion to $9 billion in new money would be needed. A tax on hospital revenues is proposed as the major source of new funds.

The system would end the categorical approach to providing medical services to the poor and would offer instead a true safety net to all citizens who are or become poor. That would be accomplished by accepting, even institutionalizing, a "two-class" system of care. It can be argued, and I will argue, that a separate system can serve the needs of the poor better than one designed to cover the whole population. But the ultimate aim would be to make the "second" class a good one, and dependable—so good and so dependable that many in the "first" class would want to join.

The needs of the poor have often been used as an argument for national health insurance, but the poor may not be particularly well served by it. In other countries a national system of insurance or provision was adopted not for the benefit of the poor, but for the benefit of the mass of the population. If the mass of the population in the United States does not want national health insurance, pursuing it as the solution to the poor's problems will only mean those problems go unsolved.

Tallon JR, Jr. A health policy agenda proposal for including the poor. *JAMA*. 1989;261:1044.

Medicaid, the nation's major program to provide health care to low-income persons, is failing to meet the health care needs of the poor. Even though the number of poor persons without access to health insurance has grown over the past decade, 11 million persons with incomes below the federal poverty level were without any health insurance in 1988, and over 50% of the poor did not qualify for Medicaid.

If Medicaid is to provide comprehensive access to services for the poor, it must be reformed so as to correct these variations. To help achieve this goal, the Health Policy Agenda Ad Hoc Committee on Medicaid recommends eight major reforms.

Thorpe KE, Siegel JE. Covering the uninsured: interactions among public and private sector strategies. *JAMA*. 1989;262:2114-2118.

This article examines the impact of two recent proposals to cover the uninsured on the cost of a Medicaid expansion. The first, an employer mandate..., would extend private sector coverage to the employed uninsured. The second, a Medicaid "buy-in," would subsidize public sector insurance for the near poor. Implementation of these proposals in isolation or jointly would result in a dramatically different distribution of costs between the public and private sectors. Their impact on the cost of Medicaid reform highlights the importance of the broader debate concerning strategies for covering the uninsured.

The cost of expanding the Medicaid program thus depends critically on a decision concerning the appropriate role of employers in providing coverage for the uninsured....The decision concerning who should provide coverage for these 16 million persons underlies the choice of a strategy for insuring the uninsured poor in this pluralistic system. It determines whether the Medicaid program will become the primary provider of insurance for the poor and possibly the near poor, or whether it will serve as a public safety net within a broader employment-based insurance system.

Welch HG. Health care tickets for the uninsured: first class, coach, or standby? *N Engl J Med*. 1989; 321:1261-1264.

The problem of providing health care for the uninsured has recently given rise to a number of proposals aimed at making health insurance more universally available. In the past year, national health insurance, a consumer-choice plan using employer-based health insurance, and an expansion of Medicaid known as the Health Policy Agenda have all been suggested. Each of these proposals devotes considerable attention to questions of cost and funding but less attention has been given to the question of what should be purchased. This commentary focuses on the question of what coverage can be provided for the uninsured and seeks to define a middle ground between the impossible (covering everything) and the unacceptable (covering nothing).

Whatever its final form, universal insurance requires that choices be made. Physicians are not inclined to make these choices at the bedside; thus it is appropriate that they be made by society. However, physicians must participate in the formulation as well as the implementation of national health policy. To be most helpful, we need to be willing to think in terms that may be somewhat foreign to our training. Three considerations are particularly important.

First, we must think in terms of budgets.

Second, we must recognize that decisions will be made with insufficient data.

Finally, we should remember that expenditures not directly related to health may be extremely important to the well-being of the poor.

Wenneker MB, Weissman JS, Epstein AM. The association of payer with utilization of cardiac procedures in Massachusetts. *JAMA*. 1990; 264:1255-1260.

To investigate the importance of the payer in the utilization of in-hospital cardiac procedures, we examined the care of 37,994 patients with Medicaid, private insurance, or no insurance who were admitted to Massachusetts hospitals in 1985 with circulatory disorders or chest pain. Using logistic regression to control for demographic, clinical, and hospital factors, we found that the odds that privately insured patients received angiography were 80% higher than uninsured patients; the odds were 40% higher for bypass grafting and 28% higher for angioplasty. Medicaid patients experienced odds similar to those of uninsured patients for receiving angiography and bypass, but had 48% lower odds of receiving angioplasty. In addition, the odds for Medicaid patients were lower than for privately insured patients for all three cardiac procedures. These findings suggest that insurance status is associated with the utilization of cardiac procedures. Future studies should determine the implications these findings have for appropriateness and outcome and whether interventions might improve care.

COMMENTARY

John E. Jones

That we have a problem in access to health care is underscored by the expanding number of Americans, now estimated to be between 31 and 37 million, who have no health insurance. Two-thirds of the uninsured are below age 24, and half of those are below age 18. Major contributing factors that have been suggested as contributing to the large number of uninsured Americans include the shift from manufacturing to service jobs, the shift from full-time to part-time jobs, and the decreased contributions toward or elimination of family coverage by employers. These changes have occurred as health costs have risen. The increasing problem of access and steeply rising costs are principal reasons that our health care system is often unfavorably compared to the systems of Canada and some European countries. Some have suggested our problem relates to our emphasis on economic individualism or even on a moralistic, punitive stance toward the poor. While this assessment would seem unfounded, a new look is needed at public access to health care systems.

In the mid-1960s, Public Law 89-97 initiated both the Medicare and Medicaid programs, significantly expanding access to health care for the old and the poor. Medicare, a national entitlement program with national standards, subsidizes hospital, medical, and some other health care expenses of those persons over 65. Medicaid, a state-level entitlement, was intended to be a joint federal-state subsidy of selected health care for the blind and disabled and for families receiving aid to dependent children. Medicaid is means tested, while Medicare is not.

As government became the largest payer of health care bills, it simultaneously came into increasing control of the health care system. Through the last 25 years, Congress has often tinkered with Medicaid, alternately decreasing and expanding eligibility limits. The Medicaid program is caught in a pinch between decision makers in Washington and the states. Furthermore, the effectiveness of Medicaid is clearly compromised by its dual responsibility to provide care for the elderly and disabled and both acute and preventive care to the poor. Today only 25 percent of Medicaid expenditures are for low-income mothers and children while 75 percent of Medicaid expenditures are for the blind, elderly, and disabled. It would appear that the outpatient and preventive care needs of the young will always yield to the institutional needs of the old.

The rising cost of health care and the deterioration of the rural economy in the past 20 years have caused further perturbations to our health care system. Today rural health care access poses particularly challenging problems since a disproportionate number of the poor live in rural areas. More than half of the rural poor are in the South and about 25 percent are in the North Central region. Rural jobs are much less likely to offer health insurance than are urban industries. Worse yet, fewer of the rural poor have Medicaid coverage than do their urban counterparts.

Poverty increases health problems through lack of access to care, lack of education about health, poor nutrition, poor housing, poor sanitation, inadequate water supplies, transportation difficulties, and inability to buy health insurance. The rural poor are also more likely to have significant chronic health problems.

Rural America has benefitted from various federal programs, which increased the number of hospitals (Hill-Burton legislation) and instituted other rural primary care initiatives such as Community Health Centers, Migrant Health Centers, Area Health Education Centers, Rural Health Clinic Reimbursement, and the National Health Service Corps. However, these 1970s rural initiatives often met only short-term needs, such as putting physicians in rural areas, and seldom provided adequate incentives for such providers to remain.

Intermediate steps such as developing a community-based coalition to achieve improvements in indigent care have been beneficial. Incremental improvements to the Medicaid program have set national income eligibility standards for pregnant women, infants, and children, as well as for the population that is eligible for both Medicare and Medicaid. Strategies developed to improve the availability of local services have included reducing barriers to services (e.g., transportation), increasing local awareness of access problems, initiating legal actions, working to improve county government's administration of services for the poor, and cooperating with academic health centers to enhance their ability to provide uncompensated care. While these approaches are helpful, they have not solved the problems.

Few would argue that the current fragmented Medicaid system for which 60 percent of the poor are ineligible is adequate. Major reforms of Medicaid have been suggested, including the development of national standards and goals, breaking linkages to public assistance programs, developing national income eligibility standards, adding cost effectiveness measures, developing policies and incentives to broaden provider participation, and having a greater burden of the fiscal impact borne by the federal government.

Proposals have been made to extend private sector coverage to the employed uninsured through an employer mandate, and to provide a Medicaid "buy in" for the near poor. These proposals would include between 20.5-24.9 million individuals at costs projected between $23.2-29.5 billion in 1989 dollars. The fundamental difficulty of implementation will be the allocation of costs between the public and private sectors.

A "two-class" system of care based on a joint federal-state system, expanded through a $6 billion to $9 billion hospital revenue "sick tax" also has been proposed by Louise Russell. Florida and New Jersey already have such hospital taxes. However, recent news from New Jersey (with a hospital tax now at 19 percent) does not smell of success. The cost for those who lack health insurance in New Jersey has risen from $399 million in 1986 to an expected $750 million in 1990. The program is said to be punishing insurers, paying patients and employer plans, and to be pushing hospitals to the brink of insolvency.

Academic health centers and their owned or major affiliated hospitals have long provided a disproportionate share of charity care. Some academic health centers receive some compensation from their states for charity care.

Our setting at a land grant university in the second most rural state in the nation provides many challenges. One of our most effective efforts was to develop strong collaborative programs with the University Extension Service to expand our capability to provide community services. Ongoing programs relate to women and children, health education, cancer, nutrition, wellness and the problems of teenage pregnancy. We provide support for care-givers throughout the state and region through a toll-free telephone consultation service that makes our specialty services readily available; this service receives more than 10,000 calls a year. Through a grant from the National Cancer Institute, we operate the Cancer Information System statewide. We provide support to many communities and practitioners by offering a number of specialty clinics staffed by faculty physicians.

Our Visiting Clinician program offers family practitioners regular opportunities to come to the academic health center to teach, serve as role models, and update their knowledge in a specialty of their choice. This also allows us to identify rural practitioners who are most interested in, and capable of, providing high-quality instruction for students on rural educational rotations. With our major affiliated teaching hospital we offer administrative and accounting support, and educational and other cost-free services to about one-third of the state's rural hospitals.

Given the troubled economic condition of our state, funding for such outreach programs has been either self-generated or provided through successful application for community-service grants from major foundations.

All academic health centers have developed innovative ways of contributing to the solutions of health care problems in their states or regions. Circumstances will likely require that we provide more service/education programs to support the poor and public health needs in our various locations.

Most proposed solutions to the current problems carefully skirt hard choices, promise to cover nearly every conceivable health service, and disregard limitations on resources. It is time for our nation to define the elements of an adequate health care plan or, put another way, to define what the plan will not cover.

We currently ration by excluding millions of people from care. Might it not be preferable to expand care to millions now deprived and achieve the required cost restraints by excluding defined services? This is, in essence, the Oregon plan. A national health policy should include priorities of health care, elements of the effectiveness of care and cost (and the allocation of same to the public and private sectors), and realistically deal with expenditures that may not directly relate to health but might be more important to the poor, such as housing.

For rural care, while improvements on reimbursement for rural hospitals and primary care physicians are desirable and may help, the fundamental problem of chronic poverty and its myriad accompaniments must be addressed if lasting solutions are to be found. It is unlikely that either the federal or state governments will rush to tangle with this problem.

Russell L. Miller, Jr.

During the past few years a great deal of attention has been focused on the issues governing access to health care. These are powerful issues because they are partial determinants of which patients will live and the quality of their lives. The focus on the barriers to access is well placed because the United States spends more of its gross national product on health care than any other industrialized nation. Yet, the number of individuals and families who are medically indigent has reached unacceptable levels and the number continues to increase. The uninsured as a percentage of the American population under 65 increased from 14.4 percent in 1980 to 17.8 percent in 1987. Worse yet, one-third of the medically indigent are children.

The problems of access are diverse and invariably include patients who have one or more of the following characteristics: poverty; belonging to a racial minority; being very young; suffering from a catastrophic illness or one that requires long-term care; possessing government health insurance; providing self-payment for health care; or living in a rural or a central urban area. Many of the same characteristics can be observed in the patients that are served by hospitals that have closed or are in danger of closing because of finances. In a nation that espouses the credo that no one should be denied health care because of inability to pay, it is ironic, but not surprising, that the current fragmented, expensive, and budget driven system for providing health care to those who cannot afford it should have erected such formidable barriers to access.

In spite of well-intentioned efforts by the federal government to develop more responsible health care programs and to remove barriers to access, many of the federally-sponsored programs such as Medicaid have remained fragmented and expensive. For example, there are over 35 federal health programs in the 16 different agencies that serve children. The administrative costs must be enormous for managing these separate programs in so many different agencies in order to serve the same population of patients. Coordination and evaluation of the programs and benefits is almost impossible. Even if the problems related to fragmentation could be resolved at the federal level, similar problems will continue to serve as barriers to access at the state and local levels.

Medicaid and Medicare were designed initially to be the health care safety nets until national health insurance legislation was passed. The Medicaid program was never intended to provide universal health coverage for the uninsured and underinsured. It was established to insure individuals who were eligible for cash grant programs, including Aid to Families with Dependent Children and Supplemental Security Income/State Supplementation Programs. For working-age adults and their children, eligibility for Medicaid is contingent upon being destitute. It is clear that the Medicaid and Medicare programs were much more expensive than predicted initially. The rapid increases in the costs of these programs have had two far-reaching consequences. First, early proposals that would have replaced the Medicaid and Medicare programs with a national health insurance program died quickly and quietly. The second effect has been the implementation of a number of other government-sponsored programs to control health care expenses. These control measures, however, added regulatory burdens and have become additional barriers to access while only moderating the increase in costs.

As the government has attempted to limit the resources required by Medicaid and Medicare, these programs have become more and more budget driven. Attempts to control the demand on the resources for these sponsored programs have depended largely on restrictions of eligibility and provider payments. The desire to control health care costs has become so acute that the interests of the patient have often become secondary. By 1986, Medicaid covered less than half the impoverished population in 29 states. It seems that the Medicaid program has become a zero net sum activity; as the Congress legislates expansion of the program, many of the states limit the eligibility and/or rates of reimbursement. Currently, our society seems to have embarked on a program of rationing of health care because of economic considerations. The rationing policies are threatening access to the system for those who need access to health care most. A way must be found to provide a minimum level of access and services to all who need it. The cost reduction aspects of rationing could then be focused more appropriately on the need for coverage of certain high-cost services that may not need to be routinely available.

As they have become the safety net for health care for their respective communities, many teaching hospitals have reluctantly assumed the role that the government traditionally has been expected to play. A growing elderly population suffering from more chronic illnesses, coupled with changes in the reimbursement pattern, has generated the need for additional long-term care beds and medical services in nursing homes. Until the long-term care need is met, hospitals are often required to provide a significant amount of care for which they will receive no compensation. The emergency rooms of hospitals have become the major source of care for many uninsured and underinsured patients.

The use of hospital facilities for care disproportionally affects minority patients. A large number of minority patients must rely on hospital clinics and emergency rooms for primary care. For example, the National Center for Health Statistics reported that 27 percent of blacks compared to 13 percent of whites stated that a hospital clinic or emergency room was their usual source of care. The problems have been made worse in recent years because hospitals can no longer remain competitive by engaging in cost shifting. Several medical centers have been pushed to the financial brink because of the large amount of uncompensated care that they provide. As more hospitals experience financial difficulties and close, the burden of uncompensated care shifts to fewer hospitals. The survival of each of the remaining institutions will be jeopardized unless access to care by poor patients is limited. When hospitals limit access, many poor patients lose their major source of health care. There is strong circumstantial evidence that the recent increases in the barriers to access for health care from conception to old age for blacks are directly linked to the decreasing life expectancy of black males in this country.

Availability and capacity of health care resources are formidable barriers to access. In rural and central urban areas the issues become important limitations. Uneven access to health care caused by geographic maldistribution of facilities and providers in rural areas and inadequate capacity in central urban areas is unacceptable for a society that has devoted a great deal of energy and resources to study perceived excess of physicians and inpatient facilities.

There have been a number of proposals put forward to remove some of the barriers to access. A number of them involve expansion and improvement of the Medicaid program. It has been suggested that Medicaid should have uniform national standards for eligibility and for reimbursement of covered services, thereby ensuring that the program is a true safety net to all citizens who are or who will become poor. Under the most conservative estimates, the proposed changes will cost at least $9 billion in new money. Other proposals have suggested that an entirely new and different approach such as a national health plan should be tried. A national health plan may cost $70 billion in new money.

Before any of the proposals receives serious consideration, a number of important issues should be resolved. First of all, what are the goals that we want to accomplish? Is it optimal health care or adequate care (a safety net)? If the goal is adequate health care—then what services should be covered? Given the fact that Medicaid was never meant to provide all poor patients or all underinsured patients access to health care, should the Congress try to tinker with existing programs or develop a bold, effective, creative new program? Why did the cost for the current government-sponsored programs rise so high so quickly? Although the causes for the increases in costs are likely to be multiple, we should know and understand the contribution of each factor before the current programs are expanded or new programs initiated. What has been the impact of potential tort liability on access to health care? Can a national health care program be developed in which the roles of physicians as gatekeepers and patient advocates are merged?

Our society and, most of all, the medical profession must develop and promote a system of care that abandons the concept of patient care activities as units of labor (mill or factory piecework) and physician behavior that reflects economic individualism. The education of students and trainees in the health professions is seldom discussed as an issue related to access. The positive role that educational activities play in expanding access throughout the nation has not been fully acknowledged. Any additional limitations on educational reimbursements may have significant negative effects on access. Although the development of a uniform nationwide health care program should be a national priority, recognition of the local barriers to access and the necessity for significant local flexibility to address these barriers will be essential to any program.

Finally, the consequences of doing nothing will be substantial in the costs of human lives and this fact must be considered when weighing the monetary costs of taking positive actions. All academic health centers will find that in order to survive with the reimbursement from current budget driven programs, limitations must be placed on the level of services provided, the amount of services provided, or the number of patients served. Patients who are uninsured or underinsured (whether by public or private payers) will find that they are confronted by increasing barriers that prevent them from gaining access to needed care.

COMMENTARY

Richard A. Matré

I
n the United States today, there are major inequalities in the accessibility to health care. Accessibility to health care is greatly influenced by its availability, affordability, and acceptability. Despite major advances in medical science and technology, there is a growing dissatisfaction among many groups of citizens with the high cost, the unavailability of services and the lack of personal responsiveness by health care providers. A recent Harvard-Harris nationwide survey found that 60 percent of the respondents felt that fundamental changes are needed in the nation's health care system while another 29 percent believed that the system must be completely rebuilt.

Although health care accounts for almost 12 percent of the gross national product, and the health care sector employs nearly eight million persons, the United States is the only Western industrialized nation without a comprehensive, national, health care delivery system. Although per capita spending in the United States for health care is higher than in other industrialized nations, we rank poorly in terms of life expectancy, infant mortality, and crude mortality rates.

Qualitatively, it is the poor of our nation who suffer the most from inequalities of access resulting from the present system of health care. It is the poor who are most often uninsured, who find care as well as caregivers unavailable and unresponsive to their needs.

Access to health care is influenced by availability not only of actual services, but also by the times services are offered. In addition, the availability of providers, the distance one must travel, and the availability of transportation are also factors. These issues are exacerbated for the nation's 8.5 million rural residents who lack health insurance.

Health care spending is escalating at an unsustainable rate. Now exceeding $604 billion or 11.6 percent of the total nation's gross national product, it is outstripping the financial resources of all of our traditional payor groups, including government and business.

Because of the high cost of health care, health insurance is becoming less available because it is less affordable, and it is less affordable because health care costs so much. This vicious circle has resulted in the inability of many Americans, mostly poor and near poor, to afford health insurance coverage. Today in the United States, 31-37 million people lack health insurance. Another 20 million are underinsured, lacking any semblance of comprehensive coverage. Fewer than one-half of the uninsured are covered by Medicaid, and a large number of these are children.

While the uninsured get a substantial amount of health care, there is evidence of the following:

- they are less healthy than insured persons of the same age, sex, race, and income;
- they pay for one-half of their care out-of-pocket;
- they use two-thirds of the care of insured persons with similar socio-demographic status;
- they appear to postpone or forego care more often than the insured; and
- they are less likely to have a regular physician than are their counterparts with insurance.

Although the Medicare and Medicaid programs have improved accessibility to health care for the poor and elderly, they have failed to provide an acceptable solution. The Medicaid program's failures result from its fragmented nature, with differing state eligibility requirements and benefit options that vary from state to state.

The poor, the uninsured, and those with public entitlement often find health care services to be unacceptable. Although services might otherwise be available, the attitudes of many health care providers toward these groups constitute a barrier to access.

Sociocultural factors, such as minority status, old age, homelessness, personal hygiene, education, income, and social class often create attitudinal barriers between physicians and providers. In addition, a sizable number of people, particularly the elderly, forego "charity" care because of perceived social stigma.

These problems are not new! Alarming as these consequences are, they have been with us for several decades. In the 1960s, Medicare and its stepchild, Medicaid, were to have solved the problems of accessibility for the poor and the elderly. In the 1970s, we concerned ourselves with rural health care, sociocultural correlates to access, and spiraling health care costs. And, in the 1980s, we focused on health manpower shortages, technology diffusion, and new health care financing and organizational systems, many of which were based on private sector initiatives.

It seems as if we have come full circle. We are still talking about how, as a society, we can provide access to health care services to all our citizens. We have not yet come far enough to seriously address the issues of what services and at what level of quality services should be made available for those who cannot afford to pay.

The papers included in this chapter of the book clearly document the problems related to access, and eloquently argue for reform. But, how is reform to be accomplished? There is no shortage of proposals, ranging from accepting the status quo to providing universal insurance for everyone. With respect to the latter, we can take our choice from several alternatives, that run the gamut from employer mandates, to rationing, to vouchers and tax credits.

The choices have become so complex that choosing one proposal over another is extremely difficult, and somewhat dependent upon one's ideological orientation. Whatever proposal ends up being adopted, it is clear that it must address issues to access, including availability, affordability, and acceptability. In addition, it must ensure that national standards are created, equality is maintained, and quality controlled. Furthermore, we cannot fall into the trap of believing the rhetoric that there will not be a significant financial cost associated with provision of universal health care services. We need only look to the lessons provided by the Medicare and Medicaid programs. These programs have cost more than anyone had predicted. And, even if net health care costs do not increase significantly, as most program advocates claim, major cost shifting will create new financial burdens for either employers or federal and/or state and local governments. It is questionable whether employers, especially small employers, or the tax payers can bear additional health care costs.

How then are we to proceed? The answer is with extreme caution, on a solid foundation of research, and with as much national consensus as can be mustered. What will hopefully emerge will be a program that will provide all Americans with access to those health care services necessary for the development and maintenance of life and well being at a price we can afford, while eliminating barriers to access based on availability, affordability, and acceptability. A tall order, but we owe ourselves no less.

COMMENTARY

W. Douglas Skelton

A ccess to health care is receiving much attention today. Such attention is appropriate, and the intensity of concern perhaps long overdue. The public, political leaders, and leaders of medical and health care organizations have been seeking and support, to greater or lesser degrees, access to affordable, quality health care for all Americans. Before reflecting on specifics of the problem and approaches to resolution, it should be recognized that considerable improvement in access to care has occurred over the last 25 years. There has been an increase in the number of Americans seeing a physician, as well as increases in life expectancy, survival rates for many diseases, and society's attention to such matters as AIDS, geriatric care, and rural health issues. The problems that remain need to be solved by Americans working together, fully recognizing the accomplishments of the past, to close the gaps in care.

The articles on access reference many groups, including children, rural residents, the poor, the elderly, and AIDS patients, and focus our attention on targeted responses. Our country has seen many specific groups benefit from targeted approaches. The larger the group and the stronger the national will, as measured by dollars, the better the results. Local efforts for AIDS patients, a rural community, or any other group will flounder when financing is no longer available. A national example of such an occurrence was the loss of mental health services for the poor when federal grants were withdrawn. The reality of a payroll always tends to focus our attention.

So, concern about access is not new. Will the current concern result in changes of the magnitude, in terms of providing access to those now left out, as did the Medicare and Medicaid programs? I am optimistic for three principal reasons. First, the country is beginning to understand that a large portion of those in need are our neighbors, that is workers and their children. Second, there are increasing amounts of data available regarding the association between the ability to pay and the availability of services. Cardiovascular services and cesarean sections have been studied in terms of provision of service based on economic distinctions. Such issues raise questions about the appropriateness of care for the poor. And third, the growing recognition that other industrialized countries have been able to provide access to all their citizens while preserving many of the values we hold dear, such as freedom of choice of physician.

It seems to me the health access proposal of the American Medical Association contains many of the essentials, including uniform benefits to all below the poverty line, employer provision of insurance to full-time employees and families, coverage for the medically uninsurable, professionally developed practice parameters to ensure appropriate care, broader risk sharing in insurance plans, and expanded federal support for medical education and research.

CHAPTER X
Rationing Health Care

ABSTRACTS AND EXCERPTS

Aaron H, Schwartz WB. Rationing health care: the choice before us. *Science*. 1990;247:418-422.

Rapid technological advances and upward pressure on wages of hospital personnel are leading to a steady increase in health care spending that is absorbing an ever-larger fraction of gross national product. Eliminating inefficiencies in the system can provide brief fiscal relief, but rationing of beneficial services, even to the well-insured, offers the only prospect for sustained reduction in the growth of health care spending. The United States, which has negligible direct experience with rationing, can learn about choices it will face from the experience of Great Britain where health care has been rationed explicitly for many years.

The term "rationing" is used in two distinct senses. First, market economies persistently deny goods to those who cannot afford them. All goods, including health care, are rationed in this sense, especially for the poor and some others who face large expenses and lack insurance. Such price rationing of medical care has a long and, in our view, ignoble history in the United States. This problem affects about 15 percent of all Americans. Second, the term "rationing" is used to refer to the denial of commodities to those who have the money to buy them. In this sense sugar, gasoline, and meat were rationed during World War II. The question now being raised is whether health care should be rationed in this sense, whether its availability should be limited, even to those who can pay for it. This kind of rationing would affect the 85 percent of all Americans who currently have health insurance and any others who may later be added to their ranks. While the first question is urgently important, we shall be focusing on rationing in the second sense.

Concern for fundamental values such as age, visibility of an illness, and aggregate costs of treatment will inevitably shape our decisions on resource allocation. Physicians and other providers will increasingly experience tension between their historic commitment to doing all that is medically beneficial and the limitations imposed on them by increasingly stringent cost limits. And we can almost certainly expect a substantial fraction of our society, much larger than in Britain, to use whatever means are available to get care that is in short supply. Whether we allow a separate hospital sector to develop outside the constrained system will be a key policy issue and a difficult political decision.

Callahan D. Rationing medical progress: the way to affordable health care. *N Engl J Med.* 1990;322:1810-1813.

Reprinted with permission of *The New England Journal of Medicine.*

There is considerable agreement on the outline of the problem: we spend an increasingly insupportable amount of money on health care but get neither good value for our money nor better equity in terms of access to health care. Greater efficiency and greater equity are widely accepted as goals in response to our troubles. They are being pursued through cost-containment efforts on the one hand, and proposals for universal health care on the other.

In any case, we must be prepared to ration medical progress and in particular to forgo potentially beneficial advances in the application and development of new techniques. I am not proposing a diminution of efforts to extend our store of theoretical biologic and medical knowledge. A strong commitment to basic biomedical research remains an attractive and desirable goal. That commitment is not incompatible, however, with several insistent requirements: (1) that clinical applications be subjected to stringent technological assessments before dissemination; (2) that the social and economic standards for the assessment be biased toward restrictiveness ("strait is the gate and narrow the way" might be a pertinent maxim here); and (3) that it is understood and accepted that some, perhaps many, beneficial applications will have to be passed over on grounds of cost and other, more pressing social priorities.

Whether we like modifying our basic values or not, it seems impossible to achieve equity and efficiency without doing so. Having a minimal level of adequate care available to all means that if such care is to be affordable, it must be combined with limits on choices, progress, and profit. Setting limits means we cannot have everything we want or dream of. The demand for priorities arises when we try to live with both decent minimal care and limits to care. At that point we must decide what it is about health care that advances us most as a society and as individuals.

Grumet GW. Health care rationing through inconvenience: the third party's secret weapon. *N Engl J Med.* 1989;321:607-611.

Reprinted with permission of *The New England Journal of Medicine.*

Many strategies for the containment of medical costs have emerged from systems of managed care—gatekeeping by a primary care physician, prior authorization and utilization review, assumption of financial risk through capitation payments to the provider with financial disincentives for hospitalization or referral to specialists, and so forth. But another feature has crept into the managed care formula and has been largely overlooked: that of slowing and controlling the use of services and payment for services by impeding, inconveniencing, and confusing providers and consumers alike.

American health care is now controlled haphazardly and is financed by multiple cumbersome, poorly integrated bureaucracies in desperate need of coordination, simplification, and streamlining. Perhaps the emerging Joint Commission on Accreditation of Healthcare Organizations can play a part by rewarding insurers who simplify and streamline operations, and by penalizing obstructive carriers. The methods of medical cost containment that we choose to invoke must be rational, explicit, equitable, and free of ambiguity, deception, or harassment.

Jecker NS, Pearlman RA. Ethical constraints on rationing medical care by age. *J Am Geriatr Soc.* 1989;37:1067-1075.

Reprinted with permission from the American Geriatrics Society.

In a statement published in this issue, the Public Policy Committee of the American Geriatrics Society endorses the view that chronological age should not be a criterion for exclusion of individuals from medical care. This article aims to amplify the Committee's position by placing it within a broader context and identifying its justification in ethical argument. The paper is divided into three parts. The first part clarifies the difference between allocation (the distribution of funds between categories) and rationing (the distribution of funds within a single category). It is argued that given the current allocation of funds to medical care, some form of rationing is unavoidable. As others have noted, rationing is already occurring in an informal and piecemeal fashion. However, ethically sound rationing requires publicly debated and defensible policies. The second section of the paper reviews a number of arguments advanced in favor of rationing medical care on the basis of age. Objections to these arguments are carefully set out. The final part of the paper details and defends a series of positive arguments establishing special duties to the elderly. The paper concludes that to the extent that scarcity forces rationing, older persons should not be excluded because they are old.

Levinsky NG. Age as a criterion for rationing health care. *N Engl J Med.* 1990;322:1813-1815.

Reprinted with permission of *The New England Journal of Medicine*.

A widely held view is that medical costs are a problem verging on a crisis. Perhaps on the principle that drastic problems require drastic solutions, for the first time powerful voices have been raised in favor of explicit rationing as a solution—possibly the only solution—to the looming cost crisis. And, in a remarkable reversal of recent history, age has been proposed as a criterion for withholding medical care. This has occurred in a society that less than 30 years ago established Medicare, its first national health plan, specifically to improve the health of the elderly.

Why have the elderly become the focus of proposals to reduce the cost of health care in America? A number of factors appear to be involved. Enthusiasm for eliminating lifesaving care for the elderly may derive as much from the attitudes of Americans toward the old as from the real pressures of rising health care costs. Social commentators have long noted the emphasis on youth and the devaluation of the aged in American society. Another factor may be a perversion of the movements for patient autonomy and "death with dignity."

Should American society decide to ration explicitly, I would argue strongly against using age as a criterion. Only if routine medical care were withheld would the savings be substantial. The noneconomic costs of a national policy to restrict routine care for the elderly would be high....If rationing is only the impersonal application of a rule to a faceless group, we risk an ever-expanding set of exclusions of the elderly from medical care as costs increase.

Morell V. Oregon puts bold health plan on ice. *Science.* 1990;249:468-471.

Oregon's commission thought it had the solution....A means had been found, the stories went, to assign a cost-benefit rating to nearly 2000 medical procedures. The basis of the list was a mathematical formula. All that had to be done was to feed piles of data into a computer, and the machine would respond with a list of procedures, carefully ordered according to their cost-benefit ratios.

Sounds great. But the list the computer actually spit out last May left the 11 commissioners reeling. Take thumb-sucking and acute headaches. Treatments for these problems ranked higher than those for cystic fibrosis and AIDS. Immunizations for childhood diseases did not appear. Deeply embarrassed, the commissioners hastily withdrew the list....a revised list is not expected until some time in the fall.

The traumatic Oregon experience might serve as an object lesson for the entire nation in the complexities of trying to simultaneously achieve equity and contain health care costs.

But the quid pro quo here was that the state would no longer finance all medical procedures—only the ones that had the highest ratio of costs to benefits.

But as the commission, along with Kitzhaber and his allies, discovered, deciding how to rank health care treatments is no simple task. The procedure Oregon hit on combined community values—as described by Oregonians themselves—with a mathematical technique for estimating costs and benefits.

These findings—which indicated the Oregonians generally favor preventive health care—were then mathematically correlated with cost-benefit data for various medical procedures to produce the controversial list.

...the plan's critics argue that the scheme will work against exactly those whom it is intended to help, the poorest and most defenseless part of society—in particular, poor women and children.

...Oregon's exercise in rationing may be seen as either a grand experiment or a crazy aberration. But if nothing else, it has stirred the pot in a national debate that won't go away: health care reform.

Priester R, Caplan A. Ethics, cost-containment and the allocation of scarce resources. *Invest Radiol.* 1989;24:918-926.

Reprinted with permission of *Investigative Radiology.* Copyright 1990: J. B. Lippincott Co.

Rationing can take place at many different levels of decision-making; when rationing is the strategy used to respond to scarcity in health care settings, it carries consequences of tremendous moral importance.

The distribution of health care resources occurs at three distinct levels: (1) between health care and other social expenditures; (2) within the health care sector, and (3) among individual patients. It might be useful to refer to the first two levels of distributional problems as "macroallocation" and to refer to the third level of distribution as "microallocation."

The intertwined issues of costs and access underlie America's health care crisis. Strategies to address this crisis generally are based on two principles: (1) health care resources ought [to] be used efficiently and (2) resources ought [to] be distributed equitably. There is no consensus, as yet, on whether our health policies should focus on cost and access simultaneously, or give cost containment top priority, or first assure all Americans have access to health care and only then worry about cost containment.

Equity in the distribution of health care resources at the level of macroallocation has alternatively been said to require (a) strict egalitarianism, (b) access based solely on medical necessity, (c) access to an adequate or minimal level of care, or (d) equal opportunity. Others have suggested that our nation can achieve equity in macroallocation by instituting rationing policies that utilize (e) age or (f) personal responsibility to limit access to health care.

From the point of view of health care, it would appear that the primary goal of medical care should be to provide benefits to those in need. The principle that should guide rationing is that health care providers should minimize the role of extraneous factors such as race or gender and strive to pursue distributional policies that have the greatest chance of providing the greatest benefit for the greatest number.

What is fair in microallocation need not be seen as fair in macroallocation; what is obvious is that rationing is a distributional policy to be earnestly avoided at any level of allocation.

Relman AS. The trouble with rationing. *N Engl J Med.* 1990;323:911-913.

Suddenly everyone is talking about rationing....rationing is now widely advocated as the only effective way to control health care costs.

The argument goes like this: An aging and growing population, rising public expectations, and the continual introduction of new and expensive forms of technology generate a virtually unlimited demand for medical services, which inevitably exhausts the resources we are wiling and able to devote to health care. Sooner or later we will be forced to limit expenditures by restricting services, even those that are beneficial. Of course, we are already restricting services through our failure to provide health insurance to many who cannot afford it, but we now must confront the necessity of explicitly denying certain services to insured patients—at least to those whose insurance is subsidized by government or business.

Our cost crisis, and the limitations on access that result from high costs, stem from an inherently inflationary and wasteful health care system. Rationing is not likely to be successful in controlling costs unless we deal with that basic problem. Given the huge sums we are now committing to medical care as compared with other developed countries, we should be able to afford all the services we really need, provided we use our resources wisely. Concerted attempts to improve the system rather than ration its services are the next sensible step. Even if reform of the system should prove to be an insufficient remedy, it would still be necessary for the ultimate acceptance and success of any rationing plan.

COMMENTARY

James E. Dalen

O n the first day of classes for the incoming freshman medical students at the University of Arizona this fall I asked, "How many of you have had a physician advise you not to enter medicine?" Nearly every student raised his or her hand. I then asked, "How many of those physicians were your mother or father?" Eight to ten hands were raised. Such a response would have been unthinkable when I entered medical school.

The principal reason for this manifest discontent by American physicians is, in my opinion, the result of our attempts to contain the costs of medical care. DRGs, PROs, PSROs, HMOs, PPOs, and their kindred have failed to contain the costs of medical care. But they have succeeded in making the practice of medicine far less satisfying than in the past. Unless we are successful in containing health care costs, the practice of medicine in the future will be even more regulated and even less satisfying.

Given the failure of a wide variety of techniques to control health care costs, many have concluded that we must ration health care.[1-3] Aaron and Schwartz[4] have defined rationing of health care, saying that "not all care expected to be beneficial is provided to all patients."

If we are to ration health care, what shall be the basis? One of the most commonly suggested criteria is on the basis of chronological age.[5-7] Given the fact that the elderly are the heaviest users of health services it is not surprising that they are a prominent target. Some argue that using high technology to prolong life in terminally-ill, elderly patients is inappropriate. It may well be. If it is, it is just as inappropriate in terminally-ill patients who are not elderly. To withhold or ration medical care on the basis of chronological age would be as discriminatory as withholding care on the basis of sex, color, or creed.[8]

Another potential basis for rationing is on ability of the patient, or more likely his or her "payer," to pay. The Medicare and Medicaid programs helped to break down financial barriers to health care. Does any responsible physician or citizen want to return to the era of charity care? I believe that we can help to contain health care costs by rationing, but rationing on the basis of efficacy. We do not have to withhold appropriate beneficial care. We need only to consider withholding care that has been proven to be of no value or furnishes so little benefit as to be inappropriate.

Multiple studies have shown that many diagnostic and therapeutic procedures are inappropriate; that is, they do not benefit specific patients. It is difficult to estimate the cost of these inappropriate procedures, but the total cost must be staggering.

Often new procedures are reported in the literature and introduced before the efficacy and appropriate indications for use have been assessed and evaluated. Thus procedures often become incorporated into physicians' practice patterns with only minimal data available to determine in which patients or under what circumstances the procedure may be of most benefit. In the examples that follow, I have chosen procedures in cardiology, my own field of expertise, for which the efficacy needs to be assessed. A similar look at other areas of medicine will reveal, I am sure, similar findings. Physicians' practice patterns with regard to the use of procedures will be difficult to change. Perhaps we should start with the way we introduce new procedures. When new procedures are introduced, we should evaluate them in the same manner that we evaluate new drugs. We should insist that the specific indications, that is, the circumstances under which we can expect a given patient to benefit from the procedure, be delineated before reimbursement is authorized.

A case in point is the use of the pulmonary artery catheter for bedside hemodynamic monitoring. This technique, introduced in 1970,[9] allows the physician to measure cardiac output, right heart pressures, and left ventricular filling pressure, at the bedside. In 1990, it was estimated that two million Americans undergo this procedure each year. Given average charges of $502 per patient for this procedure,[10] the total charges would be $1 billion per year. Yet the appropriate indications for this procedure are still uncertain. One of the most common uses has been in assessing patients with complications of acute myocardial infarction. Two different studies that involved thousands of patients could find no evidence that pulmonary artery catheterization benefits patients with acute myocardial infarction as measured by case fatality rate, length of hospital stay, or long-term prognosis.[11-13] Furthermore, a recent study of physicians using this procedure found that "physician understanding of the use of pulmonary artery (PA) catheterization is extremely variable and frighteningly low."[14] I do not suggest that we ban the use of the PA catheter. It is a very useful procedure for the right patient in the right clinical setting.

However, we need to clearly define the circumstances under which this and all other procedures can be expected to benefit an individual patient. As pointed out by Relman,[15] we need to consider "personalized rationing," a formidable task.

In a study of the use of diagnostic procedures in patients with acute myocardial infarction over a 10-year period, we found that the use of new diagnostic procedures increased at an incredible rate.[10] From 1975 to 1984, among all patients hospitalized for acute myocardial infarction at 16 hospitals in central Massachusetts there was an increase in those who underwent specific diagnostic procedures as shown in Table X.1. In 1975, only five percent of patients had one of the four noninvasive procedures (i.e., echocardiagram, exercise testing, Holter monitoring or radionuclide ventriculography). In 1984, 70 percent of patients had at least one of these studies, and 46 percent had at least two of these procedures. There was no difference in the severity of illness between 1975 and 1984, as judged by the incidence of hypotension, cardiogenic shock, or congestive heart failure. The increase in the use of these diagnostic tests was clearly due to a change in physicians' practice patterns.

A survey of practicing cardiologists in 1984 demonstrated that the use of these diagnostic tests by practicing cardiologists throughout the

---

Table X.1
Changes in the Use of Diagnostic Procedures in Patients with Acute Myocardial Infarction

	1975	1984	P
Number of Patients	763	689	
Procedure			
Echocardiogram	2.5%	15.3%	< .001
Exercise Testing	.1%	40.3%	< .001
Holter Monitor	1.0%	34.0%	< .001
Coronary Arteriography	3.1%	9.8%	N.S.
Pulmonary Artery Catheterization	7.2%	19.9%	< .001
Radionuclide Vetriculography	2.6%	52.7%	< .001

United States was very similar to the usage in central Massachusetts.[16] The annual charges for the use of these tests was estimated to be $599 million in 1984. Yet there is no evidence that the use of these new diagnostic tests benefitted patients as judged by case fatality rate, length of stay, or long-term survival.

The specific indications for these procedures remain to be defined. Until we define the circumstances when these and other procedures can be expected to benefit individual patients, we will continue to waste valuable resources and continue to escalate the cost of health care.

Elimination of procedures that have not been shown to benefit specific patients is a form of rationing that can be accepted by physicians and their patients. The potential to reduce the costs of medical care by billions of dollars is clearly evident.

REFERENCES

1. Aaron H, Schwartz WB. Rationing health care: the choice before us. *Science.* 1990;247:418.
2. Callahan D. Rationing medical progress: the way to affordable health care. *N Engl J Med.* 1990;322:1810.
3. Callahan D. Meeting needs and rationing care. *Law, Medicine and Health Care.* 1988;16:261.
4. Aaron HJ, Schwartz WB. *The Painful Prescription: Rationing Hospital Care.* Washington, D.C. Brookings Institution; 1984.
5. Callahan D. Setting limits: medical goals in an aging society. New York: Simon and Schuster; 1987.
6. Daniels N. Am I my parents' keeper? An essay on justice between the young and the old. New York: Oxford University Press; 1988.
7. Veatch RM. Justice and the economics of terminal illness. *Hastings Cent Rep.* 1988;18:34.
8. Levinsky HG. Age as a criterion for rationing health care. *N Engl J Med.* 1990;322:1813.
9. Swan HJC, Ganz W. Hemodynamic measurements in clinical practice: a decade in review. *J Am Coll Cardiol.* 1983;1:103.
10. Gore JM, Goldberg RJ, Alpert JS, Dalen JE. The increased use of diagnostic procedures in patients with acute myocardial infarction: a community-wide perspective. *Arch Intern Med.* 1987;147:1729.
11. Gore JM, Goldberg RJ, Spodick DH, Alpert JS, Dalen JE. A community-wide assessment of the use of pulmonary artery catheters in patients with acute myocardial infarction. *Chest.* 1987;92:721.
12. Zion MM, Balkin J, Rosenmann D, Goldbourt U, et al. Use of pulmonary artery catheters in patients with acute myocardial infarction: analysis of experience in 5,841 patients in the SPRINT registry. *Chest.* 1990;98:1331.
13. Dalen JE. Does pulmonary artery catheterization benefit patients with acute myocardial infarction? *Chest.* 1990;98:1313.
14. Iberti TJ, Fischer EP, Leibowitz AB, Panacek EA, et al. A multicenter study of physicians' knowledge of the pulmonary artery catheter. *JAMA.* 1990;264:2928.
15. Relman AS. The trouble with rationing. *N Engl J Med.* 1990;323:911.
16. Dalen JE, Goldberg RJ, Gore JM, Struckus J. Therapeutic interventions in acute myocardial infarction: survey of the ACCP Section on Clinical Cardiology. *Chest.* 1984;86:257.

COMMENTARY

Leo M. Henikoff

R ationing health care is an odious thought, so odious, in fact, that we have not begun to speak of it until recently. Yet rationing health care on the basis of ability to pay has been intrinsic in our system for a long time. Henry Aaron and William Schwartz differentiate between price rationing and rationing commodities to those who have the willingness and ability to pay for them. It is the latter kind of rationing in health care that would be new to our system and about which the current debate revolves.

A distinct difference of opinion exists within the papers presented in this chapter of *Health Care Delivery: Current Issues and the Public Policy Debate*. Arnold Relman takes the stand that by making our current system more efficient there would be enough cost savings to obviate the need for rationing of services in the classic sense. He indicates that Joseph Califano may be of the same opinion. Not all authors shared that opinion, however.

Excesses of the current system are often cited as targets for cost savings. Examples include fraud and abuse, unnecessary services (services for which there is *no* benefit), excesses in the malpractice liability arena resulting in excessive premiums, including the attendant costs of practicing "defensive medicine," high incomes of physicians, and excessive profits elsewhere in the health care marketplace. Each of these areas should receive attention, and in some the resultant savings would have significant impact on our health care delivery system. However, Aaron and Schwartz point out that "one-time savings cannot solve the cost problem." A solution to the problems in each of the previously noted areas would result in one-time savings. Yet our major problem is in the *rate* of increase in health care costs when one looks out 10 or 20 years. Figure X.1 shows the rise in health care costs in the United States and Canada as a percent of GNP with projections to the year 2010. A one-time reduction in total expenditures in 1990 would have a significant impact in that fiscal year, but would not alter the *slope* of the line over time. In other words, expenditures would continue to rise at the same rate (figure X.2). It is apparent from this analysis that we must

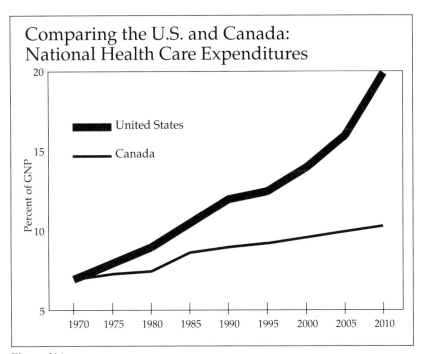

Comparing the U.S. and Canada: National Health Care Expenditures

Percent of GNP

- **United States**
- **Canada**

20

15

10

5

1970 1975 1980 1985 1990 1995 2000 2005 2010

Figure X.1

address the slope of the curve of rising health care costs. In other words, we must ascertain what is increasing at an *increasing rate*.

Certainly one factor increasing at an increasing rate is the percentage of elderly in our population. Eli Ginzberg[1] and others feel that this factor alone is of minor significance and not a major factor responsible for the increasing slope of the curve in figure X.2.

Technology is seen by some as the major culprit. Yet one must use caution in being a lumper rather than a splitter when it comes to technology. Many technologies save money in health care, and others may decrease or increase costs depending upon their use. For instance, it can be argued that magnetic resonance imaging of the head in a population of individuals exhibiting signs and symptoms strongly suggestive of brain tumor may be a cost saving diagnostic procedure when compared to other less technological methods of diagnosis. On the other hand, routine magnetic resonance imaging of the knee to verify a torn cartilage is likely to be of less value. Daniel Callahan points out appropriately that much (or perhaps most) of the new technology

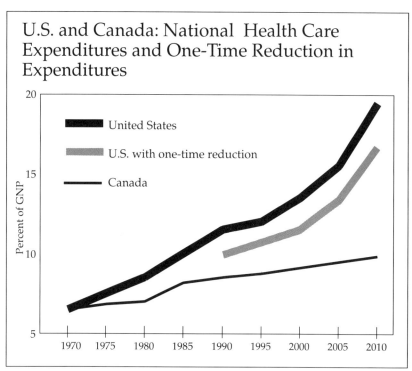

U.S. and Canada: National Health Care Expenditures and One-Time Reduction in Expenditures

Figure X.2

has accompanying benefit, but often the benefit is small in relation to the cost. There is a prevailing attitude that *any* benefit at all in health care is worth the cost it may incur. That attitude is one of the roots of the problem that leads us to the need for rationing.

Figure X.3 is a classic cost/benefit curve itself. Whereas magnetic resonance imaging for a highly suspect brain tumor may return more benefit than it costs (point A), magnetic resonance imaging of the knee to confirm a torn meniscus resides towards the end of "flat" part of the curve, where cost exceeds benefits (point B).

Value can be expressed as a function of quality, cost, and efficacy in the following equation:

$$V = Q/C \text{ x } E$$

wherein V = value, Q = quality, C = cost, and E = efficacy. By and large *value* judgments are not being made in health care delivery in the United States today. We are, in essence, buying the end of the cost/benefit curve. What is increasing at an increasing rate is the end of the curve.

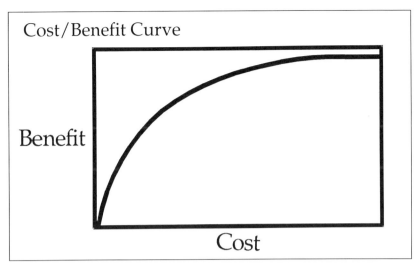

Figure X.3

Technology extends this curve at an increasing rate each year, and we collectively buy the end point as it grows.

The thesis of this commentary is in disagreement with the opinion of Relman and Califano that enough "one-time corrections" will create the savings in the system that will obviate the need for true rationing. Reinhard Priester and Arthur Caplan have summed it up succinctly in saying that "the prevailing ethic of our health care system encourages, while the legal system requires, and existing economic incentives reward, maximal levels of intervention."

The Oregon experience as reviewed by Virginia Morell describes an attempt to identify the point on the cost/benefit curve that describes adequate and appropriate health care, but does not buy "the end of the curve." Each of us looks for value, weighing costs against benefits in our choices every day. We do so when, for example, we purchase a car, a house, or decide on a university to attend. Yet it has not been our ethic to look for value when we purchase health care. Selecting the point on the cost/benefit curve that gives us the most for our money embodies the principle of selecting for value. It is clear that we as a society cannot continue to buy the end of the curve when it comes to health care. There simply is not the financial resource to do so. Therefore, we must make value decisions whether we like it or not. The Oregon approach has been the first of its kind in this regard. This reviewer feels that we as a society must make such value decisions, but that the Oregon approach was flawed in that the "list" needed much refinement before release and needed as well the inclusion of more human concerns. In addition, it has been unclear to many whether the Oregon rationing system would affect only Medicaid recipients or if it would cover the entire population. The ethic of selecting out a subgroup for rationing in this way is in question. Selecting the value point on the cost/benefit curve is a societal decision and not a decision to be made by providers alone. The Oregon approach is to be commended for its recognition of that fact and the inclusion of considerable public input into the decision-making process.

Relman sums up the question well. "This, in essence, is the health policy debate of the 1990s. Can we improve our health care system sufficiently, and soon enough, to avoid either systematic rationing or more restriction of access through pricing?" He believes the answer to be "yes" and I believe it to be "no." If the latter is true, a second question ensues, "Since we can't continue to buy the end of the cost/benefit curve in health care delivery, what is the mechanism that we shall use to pick the point on the curve that provides value and an adequate level of health care delivery for every American?"

REFERENCES
1. Ginzberg E. Personal communication.

COMMENTARY

Perry G. Rigby

Gone are the days when practicing medicine was simply a healing art. Today's practitioner is expected to understand and contend with a multitude of administrative procedures and structures that were not even conceived of when most of the physicians who are now in practice began their educations. These include a complex and cumbersome Medicaid system, health maintenance organizations, diagnosis-related groups, CPUs, swing PPOs, retrobilling, magnetic media, and direct medical education costs, to name just a few. As the scope of health care has widened to include advances in medical technology, the cost has also burgeoned. Contributing to these costs has been the growth, migration, and aging of the population, the increased prevalence of chronic diseases and disabilities, and the addition of multiple layers of bureaucracy and third-party carriers.

In the United States we spend a larger portion of our gross national product (GNP) on health care than any other industrialized nation. The proportion of GNP for health care has approximately doubled in the last 20 years, from 5.9 percent in 1965 to more than 11 percent in 1990 and is projected to reach 15 percent by the year 2000. The question arises, just what has this exorbitant price tag purchased? The consensus appears to be that we have neither good value for the money spent nor equitable access to quality health care.

Historically, many attempts have been made to curtail the growth of spending on medical care and to ensure equitable access to health services. These include the creation of the Medicare system for the elderly in 1965 and the Medicaid system to help provide health care for the poor, the 1974 congressional mandate for advanced authorization for the purchase of major equipment and facility construction (certificate-of-need), the 1984 Health Care Financing Administration reimbursement based on the diagnostic-related group (DRG) system, the creation of peer review organizations (PROs), and professional standards review organizations. It remains clear that neither the goal of cost containment nor equitable access to health care has been achieved. Each state sets its own Medicaid eligibility standards, which vary according to state budgets. While the DRG system seems to have slowed spending somewhat, it is not known how much represents economies being realized through Medicare's hospital payment system, how much is the result of shifting costs outside of the hospital setting, and how much is due to some form of rationing of health services.

Various other methods have been proposed to cut health care costs. Increasing the efficiency of our health care system by eliminating redundant medical capacity, reducing inappropriate medical procedures, (i.e., some Caesarean sections or coronary bypass surgeries performed for inappropriate reasons), increasing competition, using better management techniques, systematically assessing the effectiveness of medical technologies, emphasizing prevention, and promoting public education, are among the suggested ways to reduce costs. All of the proposals are designed to contain health care costs, improve access, maintain quality, and avoid rationing.

According to Callahan, it is not a matter of either/or. He maintains that an economically sound health care system must combine three elements: access for all to a base level of health care, a means of limiting the use of procedures that are ineffective or marginally effective as well as some of the procedures that are effective but too expensive; and some consensus on health care priorities, both societal and individual so that we can live within our means while meeting our basic health needs. Furthermore, effective cost containment entails an austerity that would have much of the weight and effect of rationing.

The fact of the matter is that informal rationing in some form already exists in the United States. There is time rationing, price rationing (the poor and uninsured cannot afford services), geographic rationing, and rationing according to anticipated clinical outcome, political contacts, or public and media pressures. Some population groups are denied care through special interest group pressures and market forces; even do-not-resuscitate orders constitute a form of rationing. It has been suggested, most notably by Grumet, that PROs and the inconvenience of dealing with third-party carriers are subtle forms of rationing.

The term rationing must be differentiated from allocating. According to Jecker and Pearlman, rationing implies a system of distributing scarce resources within a single category such as health care. Allocation has been viewed as the prior distribution of funds among different categories such as health care, defense, or education. In our present budget environment, finite funds are allocated to health care, suggesting to many the need for formal rationing within the health care system. Some observers also see the inevitability of rationing based on the fact that the money—funds to buy medical care—is limited.

Priester and Caplan note that in most cases of scarcity, health care resources are rationed at the level of microallocation—that is among individual patients, and allocated at the level of macroallocation—that is between health care and other social expenditures or only within the health care sector. While some choices imply rationing, not all decisions to allocate resources constitute rationing, and the ethical considerations of the two are quite different. What may be acceptable in terms of the macroallocation of resources may not be accepted by society in terms of microallocation decisions.

If rationing is to be imposed, the question is, what type? Shall it be explicit, where health care services are limited even to those who can afford to pay for them. This type of rationing would affect the 85 percent of the Americans who currently have health insurance as well as future members of this group. Or, shall it be implicit, like the system in place in Great Britain where public input is excluded from the process. If we adopt a formal rationing approach, what services are rationed and to whom? Is age a criterion to determine care? Should the use of and advancement of technology be rationed? What of those who will seek and buy care outside of the system? These questions force us to take a hard look at our health care system. There are good arguments that have been raised on both sides of the issue and deserve careful scrutiny. It all comes down to choices. Americans value freedom, and choice is really the issue. We cannot have it all. We must decide as a society and as individuals what we are willing to give up in order to retain a standard of health care still higher than any other in the world. It is a matter of priorities.

Meanwhile, the discussions and debates continue with new solutions proposed. It remains to be seen what happens to ideas like Oregon's effort to contain health care costs by prioritizing procedures. It is now back to the drawing board as the priority list—the mathematical formula generated—proves once again that deciding how to rank health care treatments is not a simple undertaking. Even if an acceptable ranking system can be created, there are still several challenges the plan would have to surmount. In order for such a plan to be implemented by Oregon or other states thinking of following suit, Medicaid require-ments must be waived either administratively, through the federal agency that manages Medicaid, or legislatively, through Congress. Ideas like this, and rationing systems in other countries, are resources to be examined as the United States identifies ways to create a health care system that is consistent with our cultural, economic, political, and social realities. It is likely that the solution will be evolutionary rather than revolutionary.

NOTES

NOTES

NOTES

NOTES

NOTES

NOTES

NOTES

NOTES

NOTES